In Living Color

of related interest

Making Sense of Spirituality in Nursing and Health Care Practice
An Interactive Approach
Second Edition
Wilfred McSherry
Foreword by Keith Cash
ISBN 978 1 84310 365 3

Spiritual Dimensions of Pastoral Care
Practical Theology in a Multidisciplinary Context
Edited by David Willows and John Swinton
Foreword by Don Browning
ISBN 978 1 85302 892 2

Spiritual Caregiving as Secular Sacrament
A Practical Theology for Professional Caregivers
Ray S. Anderson
Foreword by John Swinton
ISBN 978 1 84310 746 0

Spirituality and Mental Health Care
Rediscovering a 'Forgotten' Dimension
John Swinton
ISBN 978 1 85302 804 5

Spiritual Growth and Care in the Fourth Age of Life
Elizabeth MacKinlay
ISBN 978 1 84310 231 1

The Challenge of Practical Theology
Selected Essays
Stephen Pattison
ISBN 978 1 84310 453 7

Medicine of the Person
Faith, Science and Values in Health Care Provision
Edited by John Cox, Alastair V. Campbell and Bill K. W. M. Fulford
Foreword by Julia Neuberger
ISBN 978 1 84310 397 4

Nearing Death Awareness:
A Guide to the Language, Visions, and Dreams of the Dying
Mary Anne Sanders
ISBN 978 1 84310 857 3

Spiritual Healing with Children with Special Needs
Bob Woodward
Foreword by Dr Hugh Gayer, The Sheiling School Medical Adviser
ISBN 978 1 84310 545 9

Spirituality, Values and Mental Health
Jewels for the Journey
Edited by Mary Ellen Coyte, Peter Gilbert and Vicky Nicholls
Foreword by John Swinton
ISBN 978 1 84310 456 8

In Living Color

An Intercultural Approach
to Pastoral Care and Counseling

Second Edition

Emmanuel Y. Lartey

Foreword by Professor James N. Poling

Jessica Kingsley Publishers
London and Philadelphia

First published in the United Kingdom in 2003
by Jessica Kingsley Publishers
73 Collier Street
London N1 9BE, UK
and
400 Market Street, Suite 400
Philadelphia, PA 19106, USA

www.jkp.com

Library of Congress Cataloging in Publication Data
Lartey, Emmanual Yartekwei.
In living color : an intercultural approach to pastoral care and counseling / Emmanuel Y.
Lartey. – 2nd ed.
p. cm.
Rev. ed. of: In living colour. 1997.
Includes bibliographical references and index.
ISBN 1-84310-750-3 (pbk : alk paper)
1. Pastoral care. 2. Pastoral counseling. 3. Multiculturalism--Religious
aspects--Christianity. I. Lartey, Emmanuel Yartekwei. In living colour. II. Title
BV4012.2.L267 2003
253.5–dc21

2002043370

British Library Cataloguing in Publication Data
A CIP catalogue record for this book is available from the British Library

ISBN 978 1 84310 750 7

Printed and bound in the United States by
Thomson-Shore, 7300 Joy Road, Dexter, MI 48130

To
Griselda
(companion and friend)
and
Theophil Festo Nii Yartey
Henry Nii Yarboi
Emmanuel Nii Yarlai
and
Paa C.
(Charles Wesley Nii Anyaa)

Contents

List of figures

Acknowledgments

I would like to offer sincere thanks to my immediate family to whom the book is dedicated. They have endured the process of writing, and more recently the content, with Mandela-esque courage and patience. Friends and colleagues Veronika Grüneisen, Jim Poling, David Augsburger, Ed Wimberly, Archie Smith, Stephen Pattison, Werner Ustorf and R.S. Sugirtharajah have all in various ways, inspired and encouraged me. Participants on the Diploma and MA courses in Pastoral Studies at the University of Birmingham since April 1989, drawn from many nations, have sampled, criticized and been lumbered with much of the material here. I am grateful for your insights.

The International Council for Pastoral Care and Counselling and host nations for the congresses down through the years; the Association for Pastoral Care and Counselling (APCC); Race and Cultural Education in Counselling (RACE); divisions of the British Association for Counselling; Helmut Weiss of Rheinische Arbeitsgemeinschaft für Klinische Seelsorgeausbildung; the African Association for Pastoral Studies and Counselling – all are worthy of mention. Under their auspices I have had opportunities to reflect with people from across the world who are concerned about many of the issues raised in the book.

Thanks also go to the Journal of Pastoral Care Publications, Inc., for permission to adapt Figures 4.1 and 4.2.

Finally, heartfelt thanks to Judith Longman for continual encouragement and to Ruth McCurry, Leilah Nadir, Miss F. McKenzie and the team at Cassell for the editorial work and production.

The inadequacies in this ongoing process of discovery are solely mine.

Emmanuel Y. Lartey
Birmingham, June 1996

Acknowledgments (Second edition)

This second edition has come about as a result of the interest, requests and good faith of many colleagues and friends who have been a source of real encouragement to me. Alice Graham McNair of Hood Theological Seminary, David Hogue of Garrett Evangelical Theological Seminary, Teresa Snorton of the Association of Clinical Pastoral Education (ACPE), Lee Butler of Chicago Theological Seminary, Bonnie Miller-McLemore of Vanderbilt University, Pam Couture of Colgate Rochester Divinity School, Harry Simmons of Virginia Union University, Gordon Lynch of Birmingham University and Elaine Graham of Manchester University all deserve special mention in this regard.

The International Academy of Practical Theology (IAPT) and the British and Irish Association for Practical Theology (BIAPT), on both of whose executive committees I have had the privilege of serving, provided the framework for many fruitful and challenging discussions. The British Association for Counselling and Psychotherapy, and its division now called the Association for Pastoral and Spiritual Care and Counselling, need to be mentioned here for the support and interest shown by members of these organizations.

I am grateful to John Swinton, the General Editor of this series in practical theology that Jessica Kingsley Publishers are presenting, for his support and good sense. Working with Claudia Conway, Amy Lankester-Owen and Leonie Sloman of Jessica Kingsley Publishers has been a pleasant experience.

I would like to offer exceedingly grateful thanks to all my new colleagues and friends at Columbia Theological Seminary, here in Decatur, Georgia, for the warm welcome, support and encouragement I have received since arriving here in October 2001 with special thanks to Debbie Hitchcock for all your help on the computer.

Emmanuel Y. Lartey
Decatur, Georgia, August 2002

Foreword

Believers in many religions worship a God who created the foundation for everything – the smallest molecule, the newborn child, and the power of nature and nations. Confessing faith requires every believer to ask what God's care for creation means in everyday life. In this book, Lartey defines care as the expression of spirituality in relation to self, others, God, and creation. For those who are Christians, such an understanding of care has universal implications for our relationship with all people, all cultures, and all religions.

However, working out the details of this ethic of care is not easy, and Lartey's work challenges all who try to be faithful to God to do critical thinking about what we believe and how we practice care. Care always has a contested meaning in a world where religious visions compete for the loyalty of humans. Many questions arise about who is authorized to define God's care, who is adequately trained and ordained to deliver care, and what persons deserve the care of Christian communities. We must move beyond simple, mono-cultural, and individualistic notions of care to understand the complex web of care that is expressed wherever people respond to one another with empathy, love, and justice.

Care is an issue of power, that is, the development and distribution of resources for persons who need care to live a safe and prosperous life. Lartey challenges the field of Christian pastoral care and counseling to confront its own assumptions about care. For too long, pastoral care has been defined within the intrapsychic and interpersonal life of human beings. Ignored in this understanding are the structures of political and economic power that determine the norms and context for daily life. Social justice cannot be divorced from care since a just environment provides the resources that make care possible.

One of Lartey's passionate concerns is the exchange of care across religious and cultural boundaries such as Christian, Jewish, Muslim, and African Traditional Religions. Assuming God's care for all people, he asks Christians to define care in such a way that all people are included in the ethics of care. He has been criticized for de-emphasizing the Christo-centric focus of Christian faith in favor of cultural and religious relativism. Such a criticism is far from the truth because he is asking a profound question – What kind of care emerges from belief in Jesus Christ? His answer is that such care must be universal, as wide as God's care for the created world. Anything less cannot be faithful to the vision of care we know in Jesus Christ.

This opens the door for dialogue with practitioners of Judaism, Islam and African Traditional Religions (ATR) who do not find their identity in Jesus Christ. In a compelling example, he suggests that Christians might incorporate the rituals of ATR into their practices of care with Africans. Some call this syncretism and say it crosses the boundary that places him outside the Christian faith. But he answers that Christians must not be possessive about God or provincial about how God's care is expressed in human life. Rather, belief in Jesus Christ calls us to a universal care that is no less Christian when it understands the presence of God's care in all communities. This opens up interreligious dialogue and challenges the hegemony of Christian power in the contemporary world. In a time when Christianity is overly identified with the political power of the United States, a move toward a universal understanding of God's love and power is prophetic and political.

As we expand our global consciousness, Lartey's revision of the meaning of pastoral care and counseling is compelling and his challenges must be incorporated into our everyday practices of love and justice.

Professor James N. Poling

Preface

This book offers a critical introduction to the practice and study of pastoral care and counseling. Its characteristic feature is that it adopts an intercultural approach to this important field. My essential goal is to offer an introduction to what I consider a more holistic approach to pastoral care and counseling in the worldwide or global context. The book also aims at providing a resource for pastoral practitioners in a wide range of caring settings. Although books on counseling seem to be increasing in number by the month, there are relatively few books available on pastoral care that go beyond mere suggestions for pastoral practice in specific situations of need. The particular relevance of and need for this one, quite apart from the fact that it treats both pastoral care and counseling, is that it offers an approach that relates to the multicultural context in which pastoral practitioners now recognize they live.

In what follows, a broad and inclusive approach is adopted in the discussion of issues. For example, *pastoral* is not simply taken to mean 'pertaining to the ordained Christian.' Instead, much more wrestling is done with what *pastoral* might actually mean in a pluralistic, postmodern and postcolonial world context. The backdrop against which this book is set is the postmodern 'mood' of current Western discourse and the postcolonial reality of much of the so-called Third World. The term intercultural, in preference to *cross-cultural* or *transcultural*, is used to attempt to capture the complex nature of the interaction between people who have been influenced by different cultures, social contexts and origins, and who themselves are often enigmatic composites of various strands of ethnicity, race, geography, culture and socio-economic setting. An attempt is made to ensure that the discussion is informed at every point by experiences, thoughts and perspectives from different cultures, with particular emphasis, reflecting my own knowledge and experience, on continental African, diasporan-African, British and American societies. This is to enable a variety of voices to be heard on central topics in pastoral care and counseling.

The approach set out in this book has recently been hinted at in a brief survey and redefinition of cross-cultural counseling (Speight *et al.* 1991). The authors of the survey aim at broadening and deepening the current understanding of multiculturalism within counseling by moving from an investigation of superficial differences among people to 'include an investigation of conceptual systems' (p.8). The basic assertion made is that 'the current status of multi-cultural counselling is a reflection of the philosophical assumptions underlying the field' (p.9). On a definition that envisages cross-cultural counseling as a relationship in which 'two or more of the participants differ in cultural background, values and lifestyle' (Sue *et al.* 1982), Speight *et al.* (1991) argue that all counseling is cross-cultural or multicultural since all humans differ in terms of cultural background, values or lifestyle. Cross-cultural counseling, they contend, has, however, tended to be conceptualized and discussed in narrower terms referring primarily to the counseling relationship where the counselor is Caucasian and the client a member of a racial or ethnic 'minority group.' Rarely is the situation discussed where the counselor *is* the 'minority' group member (e.g. Korean counselor/white client), or where both counselor and client are from different minority groups (e.g. Mexican counselor/Filipino client). Much less attention seems to have been paid to the situation where the participants in counseling represent differences within one particular group; for example 'an upper-middle-class male African American counselor with a poor female African American client; or a Caucasian heterosexual female counsellor with a Caucasian lesbian client (Speight *et al.* 1991, p.8).

The critical question within the multicultural counseling literature seems to have been 'How can a counselor and client who differ from each other effectively work together?' Thus, the ever-burgeoning field of multicultural training was born to assist counselors in understanding those who are 'culturally different' from themselves (Speight *et al.* 1991).[1] This question is important and various attempts have been and are being made to respond to it in terms of research, training and publications (see e.g. Pedersen *et al.* 1989; Sue and Sue 1990). It is also true that the mindset evident in the way in which the question is posed has led to particular ways of responding which, as will be argued here, are not always very helpful. This book broadens the scope of the question to include 'pastoral care' and offers a reconceptualization of the prevailing paradigms by which response to the challenge of multiculturalism has been attempted.

The term *pastoral* has been used in a variety of ways. It has its usages in fields as diverse as agriculture, geography, development studies, education, as well as theology. Part of the task of this book is to explore the meanings of the term, to demonstrate what value it may have in qualifying two equally varied and multifaceted enterprises, namely *care* and *counseling*. To facilitate this exploration we will restrict ourselves to the usages that have relevance within the caring professions. To do this we will ask questions about what it has meant, ways in which it is used in the caring professions currently, and also offer some suggestions as to how it might be used in a pluralistic, multicultural world.

This book takes it as self-evident that we can no longer talk of these or any other matters exclusively in a white, middle-class, Eurocentric fashion that deliberately ignores, or else fails to realize, the normalcy of pluralism in every part of the world. The truth of the polemical statement of Black psychologists Khatib and Nobles (1977) is increasingly being realized: 'Whites or Europeans are no longer the standard by which the psychology of people is judged (p.97).

For our discourse to even begin to face the reality of the lived experience of the vast majority of people in the world today, it must attempt to include the voices of very many players – women and men; people of color as well as white; African, Asian, Caribbean, South and North American, European, Australian, Pacific; old and young. It must, whilst recognizing its limitations, seriously make an effort to be as inclusive as possible. In this book much more will be drawn on from Black[2] culture and from British culture than any other. This reflects my own knowledge and lack of experience outside those cultures. I hope the approach adopted will encourage those with more experience in cultures that are underrepresented in this book to express themselves in print.

Pastoral care has a short history but a long past. At the heart of most religious traditions lies an injunction to care, to love or to pay attention to self and others. Such teaching concerning care is very often enshrined in the training and practice of the religious functionaries who have leadership and oversight of devotees. The roots of pastoral counseling in many cultures lie in the healing and restorative activities and arts practiced by priest-healers in ancient times. Priest-healers combined the roles of therapist, community consultant, priest and physician. These traditional healers were the people to whom the perplexed and the troubled would resort for solace in their need. The expectation with which people went to them was that the traditional healer would offer words and efficacious rituals, grounded in their worldview, culture and belief structure, that would be effective in bringing about relief or else explanations and meaning to their trauma. Present-day Western pastoral counselors appear in several respects very different from their historical predecessors. However, it is the case that the needs, expectations and desires for relief which propel people into relations of counseling and pastoral care today share similar features with those in the past. In virtually all areas of the world people seek out others they believe to have some knowledge; expertise or power that they understand might help them in their quest for relief, well-being or meaning in life.

McNeill (1977) has presented a useful and informative sketch of the antiquity of pastoral care linking its current manifestation with the historical term *cura animarum* or the 'cure of souls.' Today, counseling, on the one hand of broadly psychodynamic or on the other of person-centered origin, is the major form in which pastoral care is largely understood to take place in the Western world. Moreover, this approach continues to make inroads in other parts of the world. The genesis of the psychotherapeutic counseling paradigm for pastoral care is often cited as the beginning of the recent history of pastoral care.

However, questions have been raised about the appropriateness of counseling as a model for pastoral care in societies that do not share some of the major anthropological assumptions of Western culture. More directive approaches such as are represented in the cognitive-behavior therapies, have been suggested as more adequate models for non-Western cultures. Questions have been raised about the individualism of Western approaches, even where they occur in group settings. The individualism of the West has also been criticized from within the pastoral counseling field[3] as well as from outside it by movements for congregational studies that have located pastoral counseling within the local congregation.

Another major related question, emanating more recently from the United States, but reflecting concerns expressed in Britain for many years, has to do with the extent to which resources drawn from the religious traditions of pastoral care are called upon to inform current practice. Tom Oden is a recent example of this concern that features prominently in the writings of British physician-theologian R.A. Lambourne, who died in the early 1970s.

Since 1979 when the first International Congress was held in Edinburgh, the International Council for Pastoral Care and Counselling (ICPCC), has been in existence. International Congresses have been held every four years, attempting to keep relevant questions, issues and concerns alive within the worldwide community of reflective practitioners of pastoral care. Reference is made to developments in this international movement in this book.

This book is divided into two parts. Part I (History, Theory and Practice) begins with a conceptual exploration of pastoral care. Essential elements of pastoral care as envisaged here are outlined and the important concepts of culture and 'interculturality' are introduced. The first chapter ends with a new section (in this second edition) in which a discussion of postmodernism and postcolonialism as the global frames within which the project of intercultural pastoral care takes place, is offered. Chapter 2 begins by selectively surveying some historical developments in the theory and practice of pastoral care. Chapter 3 looks at metaphors and models that are employed, and Chapter 4 raises questions first about what pastoral care hopes to achieve, and second about what resources or tools exist for the tasks.

Part II is devoted to an examination of approaches to pastoral care adopted in different parts of the world. The subtitle 'Private Care *and* Public Struggle'[4] conveys the basic orientation of the section. Chapter 5 explores counseling as an approach to pastoral care. The basic assumption here is that counseling appears to provide the major operating concepts and practices for pastoral care within the Western world. Chapter 6 explores the many liberationist approaches developed largely from the perspectives of oppressed and marginalized groups in several parts of the world. The main rationale for this is that 'liberation' serves to function as a major framing category for pastoral care in the Third World. Chapter 7 attempts to respond to the question about how different understandings and experiences of spirituality in different traditions might be related to pastoral care. Chapter 8 offers a vision of pastoral care which is informed by many voices and which seeks to examine and act in ways reflective of intercultural interaction. In this chapter, two case studies are presented illustrating some of the issues discussed. The final chapter takes this further by exploring the underlying assumptions of different approaches to pastoral care in multicultural settings, ending with a fuller explanation of how the intercultural approach espoused in the book overcomes some of the dangers inherent in the others.

Notes

1. For an important contrast, see the work of the Nafsiyat Intercultural Therapy Centre in London, documented in J. Kareem and R. Littlewood (1992).

2. By *Black* I refer to African, African Caribbean, African American peoples, as well as all 'people of color,' including Asians in Britain.

3. E.g. from the 1960s. Thornton (1964) laments the absence of genuine community; Lambourne (1969/1995) raises the same issue.

4. Taken from the subtitle of the book by Peter Selby, *Liberating God: Private Care and Public Struggle*, SPCK, 1983.

PART I

History, Theory and Practice

CHAPTER 1

Introduction to Pastoral Care

In 1964, Clebsch and Jaekle offered what proved to be a groundbreaking definition of pastoral care. This was so largely because no other work of then recent currency had examined the theory and practice of pastoral care historically. It is true to say that at that time pastoral care was still very much the 'Cinderella' of the theological course curriculum. Moreover, at that time, hardly any secular usage of the term is discernible. John McNeill (1977) explored the term *cura animarum* (cure of souls) from the earliest times BCE. Clebsch and Jaekle, restricting themselves to the Christian era, identified four principal functions, which they saw as characterizing pastoral care throughout Christian history. They went on to claim that one particular function dominated particular periods of history, although recognizing that all functions were present in all ages. In spite of this historiographically somewhat naive claim, Clebsch and Jaekle's definition of pastoral care was to set the tone of the discussion for the years to come. It is true to say that the definition they offered and indeed the publication of their book, *Pastoral Care in Historical Perspective*, marked the beginning of what may be described as the recent history of pastoral care.

> Pastoral Care consists of helping acts done by representative Christian persons, directed toward the healing, sustaining, guiding and reconciling of troubled persons, whose troubles arise in the context of ultimate meanings and concerns. (Clebsch and Jaekle 1967, p.4)

This has become more or less a standard definition of pastoral care.

In spite of its generic tone, however, the definition demonstrates the important influence of social and historical location. Apart from the specified functions of pastoral care, which we examine in Chapter 4, there are four aspects of the definition that raise significant questions. First, pastoral care is identified with helping acts. It therefore has a pragmatic focus and a somewhat messianic tone, demonstrating the pragmatism and optimism of the 1960s, especially in the US. Second, pastoral care is the preserve of 'representative Christian persons.' These are not, the authors argue, to be identified with ordained clergypersons. Rather these are persons who represent Christian faith in that they bring to bear upon problems, the insights and thinking of the Christian tradition. The discussion shows little recognition of the influence of other religious traditions, notably Judaism, on pastoral care. Indeed it suggests that 'pastoral care' is *ipso facto* a Christian term, failing to recognize that the imagery of the shepherd, most beloved of Christian pastoral carers, comes itself originally from the Jewish scriptures. While it is no doubt true that the term has been developed and most significantly used in Christian discourse, it must be borne in mind that what it signifies has been characterized and practiced to a greater or lesser degree in all religious traditions and cultures. Third, pastoral care has to do with 'troubled persons.' This problem-centered focus, with the implied problem-solving approach, has affinities with the types of therapies, educational philosophies and management techniques that seem to have appeared in the US in the 1960s. Finally, the context of the troubles focused on in pastoral care is 'ultimate meanings and concerns.' This is particularly distinctive existential theological language reminiscent of the theologian Paul Tillich, whose most influential works were written in the US in the 1950s.

American pastoral care practitioner Howard Clinebell could be regarded as a guru of Western pastoral care and counseling. His publications have circled the globe and can be found on library shelves from Fiji to Finland. His first major work was entitled *Basic Types of Pastoral Counseling: New Resources for the Troubled* (1966). This was later revised and expanded in line with growth both in his perspectives and also in the discipline. This is how he describes the enterprise in the later work:

> Pastoral Care and Counseling involve the utilization by persons in ministry of one-to-one or small group relationships to enable healing empowerment and growth to take place within individuals and their relationships... Pastoral Care is the broad, inclusive ministry of mutual healing and growth within a congregation and its community, through the life cycle. (Clinebell 1984, pp.25–26)

Among the issues that are clearly central to Clinebell are the ecclesial (i.e. Christian church) context, the importance of one-to-one or else 'small' group relationships and the focus on individuals and their relationships. What was new at the time of publication was the emphasis on growth and empowerment as well as the mutuality of pastoral care 'within a congregation and its community.' This concern is now central to all considerations of the subject. Pastoral care is now clearly seen as a communal, congregational matter. Gone from Clinebell's rendition, is the 'problem-centred' focus evident in the subtitle of the first edition, which Mills is unable to escape even in 1990 when he writes: 'Pastoral care derives from the biblical image of shepherd and refers to the solicitous concern expressed within the religious community for persons in trouble or distress' (in Hunter 1990, p.836). It is still largely the case that pastoral care is seen as an 'ambulance service.'

From the British scene Alastair Campbell (1987) offered a terse but comprehensive statement of pastoral care as 'that aspect of the ministry of the Church which is concerned with the well-being of individuals and of communities' (p.188). Campbell shares the deep concern of other British writers notably Lambourne, Wilson, Forrester, Selby and more recently Pattison that socio-economic and political forces that cause distress need to be addressed in pastoral care. In overtly theological language and within the framework offered by Clebsch and Jaekle, Pattison (1993) offers the following definition:

> Pastoral care is that activity, undertaken especially by representative Christian persons, directed towards the elimination and relief of sin and sorrow and the presentation of all people perfect in Christ to God. (p.13)

The attempt to reclaim the language of Christian theology in pastoral care is observable here. This is very much in line with the desire to reclaim the Christian heritage of pastoral care and to rescue the discourse from its psychological captivity. Important as this is, it raises as many questions as it attempts to answer. Is 'the elimination of sin' a real possibility or is this the other worldly idealism of which Christianity has been so vociferously accused? What about sorrow? Is it realistic to hold out the hope that sorrow will be eliminated from people's lives? What is actually entailed in the presentation of people 'perfect' in Christ? These exciting themes are yet to be explored in Pattison's works.

African American pastoral theologian Ed Wimberly explores *Pastoral Care in the Black Church* (1979). In this book he defines pastoral care as 'the bringing to bear upon persons and families in crisis the total caring resources of the church' (p.18). Wimberly provides a model of and for pastoral care within the Black church that emerges from traditional Black pastoral care while borrowing ideas from systems and crisis theories. In his model, the four functions of pastoral care for liberation are *worship, care, nurture* and *witness*. In spite of a focus on crisis, which seems to be the bane of pastoral care worldwide, the categories and practice of pastoral care in the Black church tradition emerge as overwhelmingly about preparing, strengthening and attempting 'to change those conditions which prevent persons from choosing healthy crisis-coping patterns' (p.79), within a framework which is communal and supportive. The communal framework is crucial. Pastoral care, especially in the Black church tradition has to do with mobilizing the resources of the total community in caring for the needs of individuals and groups. Wimberly's later books, notably *Liberation and Human Wholeness* (1986), demonstrate further the importance of social context, culture, the Black symbolic universe and biblical and African eschatology in pastoral care, especially in the African American situation.

African pastoral practitioners have sought to relate their activities and their reflections to the contextual realities they are faced with. In the wake of the colonial and early missionary experience, which was largely one in which much of African life, culture and thought was denigrated, recent movements have been attempts to rediscover and revalue traditional beliefs and practices and integrate these with the theories and practices received from the West. Postcolonial writers and workers have emphasized the imaginativeness that was present within the colonized community even during Empire days. This now blossoms into the creativity with which postcolonial pastoral caregivers engage their clients. Two authors whose works reflect this shift are Masamba ma Mpolo of Zaire and Abraham Berinyuu of Ghana.

Masamba ma Mpolo has consistently shown an interest in a core belief and experience in Africa, namely that of witchcraft and bewitchment. His models of pastoral care have therefore been ones in which there is a radical search for a 'liberating spirituality' (Masamba ma Mpolo 1994). Such spirituality takes seriously African traditional cosmologies, which in fact persist and are clearly manifest in contemporary life and thought. It also seeks culturally relevant interpretations of experienced phenomena. In addition to these, African pastoral caregivers, Masamba would argue, should recognize that forms of what Western practitioners describe as psychotherapy have existed in Africa for centuries. As such, an integration should be sought with Western concepts, some of which might prove helpful in the task of liberation. Consequently, Masamba (1991) advocates 'insight-oriented therapy' while also arguing that

> disease in Africa is thought of as also having spiritual and relational causes. It may be ascribed either to bewitchment, to the anger of mistreated and offended spirits, to possession by an alien spirit, or to broken human relations. Pastoral Counselling should therefore also use spiritual means of letting people deal with their emotional needs, even through ecstasy, rituals and symbolic representations. (p.28)

Berinyuu shares similar concerns. He attempts to be deeply rooted in the therapeutic practices and interpretations of the peoples of Africa, while dialoguing critically with and attempting to integrate Western forms of healing. For him, 'a pastoral counselor in Africa, could be defined as [a] shepherding diviner who carefully guides a sheep through a soft muddy spot' (Berinyuu 1989, p.12). Berinyuu examines processes and practices of divination in Africa and proposes that divination, in both its 'inspired' and 'deductive' forms, could be considered as an African form of therapy. He chooses Freudian psychoanalysis and Jerome D. Frank's 'persuasion healing' approach as dialogue partners in his integrationist scheme.

Berinyuu proceeds by exploring the implications of storytelling, myths and proverbs, dance and drama, and finally music, for pastoral counseling. Thus he attempts a model of pastoral counseling, and as such also pastoral care, which he calls 'psychopneumatist,' drawing on an African 'spirit-filled' universe as well as culturally recognizable symbolic forms of interaction such as proverbs and dance, in the quest for appropriate responses to the experiences of life in Africa.

Essential elements of pastoral care

It appears to me that there are five essential elements that any comprehensive definition of pastoral care needs to encompass. These would be: first, a declaration of the nature of activity it is; second, a discussion of agency that explores who are involved or engaged in it; third, an indication of how it is done which includes pointing to resources and their employment in achieving the fourth element of the definition, namely the goals aimed at; last, but by no means least, is a setting forth of motive – why people do it.

In responding to these I will now set out the essential features of a definition of pastoral care that attempts to be intercultural in its nature and scope.

1. Pastoral care is an expression of human concern through activities

In pastoral care, it seems to me, deep concern about what it is to be human is expressed. Pastoral caregivers have a concern for what meets the eye about human persons as well as what may lie deeply buried within them. This implies that there is an aspect of pastoral care that may be hidden. The 'hiddenness' lies in the heartfelt desire for humanity to be truly and fully human. It is an all-encompassing passion that all people might live to the fullest of their potential. In the Christian scriptures this is expressed in the saying of Jesus recorded in John 10:10, 'I have come that they may have life, and may have it in all its fullness.' Pastoral care has to do with the total well-being of the whole person.

This concern is expressed in activity. Various helping activities such as counseling may offer such an expression but so are celebrating, commemorating, rejoicing and reflecting, as well as mourning or being present with people at different times of life.

2. Pastoral carers recognize transcendence

People who participate in pastoral care recognize a transcendent dimension to life. They realize that there is more to life than often meets the eye. They have an awareness that power, grace and goodness are often not found in the obvious places. They recognize that there is a mysteriousness about life, which is not reducible to sociological, psychological or physiological analyses and explanations, important though these be.

This transcendence is real, although we have no objective and external means of gaining access to it and of verifying whether we are right or not. Different religious traditions have developed ways of speaking about it and have elaborated rites and rituals for signifying and participating in the recognized realities. The languages and rituals of spirituality, whether religious or non-religious, are attempts at coming to terms with it. The content of transcendence for many people is shaped by the formulations of the particular religious traditions in which they have been socialized. It is possible in terms of a given tradition to ascertain the degree of fit of any particular expressed viewpoint, and as far then as that tradition is concerned there is truth and falsehood. Different religious traditions value different understandings of 'revelation' and hold their sacred scriptures to have been given by the Deity in specific ways. Each tradition is important and has valuable insights to offer. However, we have no direct access to an objective, external standard by which all viewpoints on transcendence may be judged as ultimately true or false.

In the pastoral care spoken of in this book, religious functionaries are significant participants, although they are by no means the sole or even most important participants. There is a mutuality of participation in pastoral care. Leaders there may be, and their activity certainly merits careful study. However, being an official religious representative does not automatically confer pastoral ability. As a matter of fact, there are many who testify that those who have been of greatest pastoral relevance for them have not been the most obvious or recognized. It is crucial that we study the *pastoring function* and not simply the official pastoring functionaries. Pastoral care may be mediated through the least recognized source. Unless this reality is recognized and incorporated into the study of it, much that is of the essence of pastoral care will be lost.

There is a sense in which this recognition of a transcendent dimension to life characterizes and distinguishes the *pastoral* caregiver from other carers. This is not to suggest that the pastoral carer is superior or that his or her efforts are couched in esoteric or else overtly evangelistic terms. In point of fact, pastoral carers are not overly anxious to be distinguished from other caregivers and most often work collaboratively with others in the attempt to mediate holistic care. Their desire is not self-consciously to draw attention to themselves, or necessarily to make frenetic attempts to draw attention to the mystery they recognize; rather they possess a deep consciousness that is as suspicious of superficial or facile interpretations as it is of pretentious ones.

Black psychologist Linda Myers has identified within Afrocentric thought a conceptual framework for the quest among transpersonal psychologists for a more holistic understanding of human experience that is useful for our purposes. She describes this conceptual system as 'optimal psychology' (for a fuller discussion, see Myers 1988). In the antithesis to this system, which she describes as a suboptimal worldview, reality is divided into spirit and matter, with matter being pre-eminent. Optimal theory, on the other hand, assumes the unity of spirit and matter, with spirit being pre-eminent. The primary means of gaining knowledge within a suboptimal frame is by measuring and counting information provided by the five senses or their technological extensions. According to optimal theory 'self knowledge is the source and basis of all knowledge' (Meyers 1992, p.10). These ideas provide an important link between forms of Eastern mysticism, Hebrew synthetic thinking, modern 'paradigm shift' physics and African traditional philosophy. In Chapter 6 I will take these ideas further and offer a more detailed discussion of transcendence and spirituality, which I am arguing is crucial to our understanding of pastoral care.

I recognize that the practitioners of pastoral care in educational circles, especially in Britain, would be of the view that their practice can be distinguished from 'religious activities.' They may even contest the view that they have any 'transcendental' ideas. However many would be quite happy, in the current understanding, to term their activities as catering for the 'spiritual' needs of pupils and students, if not simply to point to their concerns with the needs and well-being of the learners beyond formal teaching activities. These efforts are to do, among others, with 'the conscious effort to help young people in one way or another to develop as persons' (for a comprehensive discussion of personal development see e.g. Pring 1985). Such an interest, which could be termed a concern for 'self-transcendence' among young people, is included in the sense in which the 'transcendent' is being used here. There is room here for minimalist, generalist or secularist understandings as well as maximalist, specialist or religious understandings of transcendence.

Intercultural pastoral caregivers then, recognize transcendence and are prepared to examine the implications of transcendence for the particularities of daily human living.

3. Pastoral care entails multivariate forms of communication

Verbal communication is very important as a way in which information is conveyed and received. However, what has been somewhat pejoratively described as non-verbal communication, is increasingly recognized as a powerful mode of communication, perhaps even of greater significance than the verbal. In intercultural pastoral care, the forms of communication present in any given society are explored to ascertain their value within the society for caring interaction.

In many cultures, indirect forms of converse are very highly valued. In Gã and Akan (West African) societies for example, the mark of maturity is the ability to use proverbs, sayings and allusions appropriately in public speech. An elder is not rebuked directly but instead is spoken to indirectly. A wise ruler can read and decipher the writing on the wall. Drama, poetry and other forms of imaginative literature may convey or mediate pastoral care of the highest order. The use of symbols such as works of creative art and sculpture has largely been ignored in the study of pastoral care. It is most often literary works that have received attention. In intercultural study, this neglect is deemed most impoverishing. Some of the most inspiring and liberating forms of discourse emanating from South and Central America are in symbolic art.

4. The motive is love

At the heart of the 'hiddenness' of pastoral care is love. The passion spoken of earlier is born of the compassion that lies at the center of the universe deep in the heart of God, so to speak. In Christian terms, 'we love because God first loved us' (1 John 4:19). Love is a thoroughly social phenomenon. Not only does it impel us into relationship with others, it also enables us to recognize injustice and to desire to do something about it.

Christianity points to *agape*, referring to the unconditional self-giving love of God, as the source and sustainer of the universe. The Christian teaching of incarnation, seeks to convey an 'enfleshing' of *agape* in a historic person – Jesus Christ – who becomes the icon and enabler of such love for and in his followers. Such self-giving love is at the heart of the Christian gospel and is the impelling force behind Christian action.

The problem, of course, is the translation of this love into actual practice. It is evident that Christians have no monopoly on loving action.

In fact, evidence is plentiful of the exact opposite, especially in Christian relations with people of other faiths. Restatement of ideals, nevertheless may be a way of refocusing and calling people to the true heart, soul and potential motivating force of their practice.

In intercultural pastoral care, love is both the motivation and the motive force. Recognizing the love of God as crucial and basic for and in the created world, intercultural pastoral caregivers seek to place themselves within this love and to become agents and conduits of it. The key is the realization that the love of God is for the whole world, created diverse and affirmed in its diversity by the creative energy of God. As such, all that is done must respect and uphold the diversity in which the whole of the world is created. All attempts to force uniformity upon a world created diverse are both heretical and damaging to the creation.

5. Pastoral care aims at prevention and fostering

Much of the literature and practice of pastoral care in the West has appeared to focus on *relief.* Pastoral care thus has a cliff-hanging or 'ambulance-service' image that is hard to escape. It would appear as if pastoral care is only needed after the devastating event has occurred. Without losing sight of the importance of relieving anxiety or trauma once it has occurred, in this study, pastoral care also aims at *preventing* distress, where possible, by creative anticipation and sensitive, non-intrusive awareness-building. This is an educative exercise of pastoral care which enables people imaginatively to explore and examine situations before they occur in order to be prepared if they were to happen. Pastoral caregivers, in this view, are also deeply involved in fostering or enabling human growth and the fulfillment of the potential of individuals as well as communities.

The definition that captures these insights, one with which I have been working for a while and which, beyond slight modification, I see no reason to change at this stage, is as follows.

Pastoral care consists of helping activities, participated in by people who recognise a transcendent dimension to human life, which, by the use of verbal or non-verbal, direct or indirect, literal or symbolic modes of communication, aim at preventing, relieving or facilitating persons coping with anxieties. Pastoral care seeks to foster people's growth as full human beings together with the development of ecologically and socio-politically holistic communities in which all persons may live humane lives. (A modification and enhancement of my definition in Lartey 1993, p.5)

Culture and interculturality

It is necessary at this juncture for me to explain briefly my understanding of a concept which lies at the heart of our discussions – that of *culture*. The term is used in very many different ways, and is one of the most complex. In relation to our study, this is so as to avoid the ambiguous, and often misleading way in which it is sometimes used, and to indicate the way it is being used here.

By *culture* I shall be referring to the way in which groups of people develop distinct patterns of life and give 'expressive form' to their social and material life experience (see Billington *et al.* 1991; Hall 1981). This way of speaking of culture has been described as an 'anthropological' one.[1] In this sense, the culture of a group of persons is the particular and distinctive 'way of life' of the group. This includes the ideas, values and meanings embodied in institutions and practices, in forms of social relationship, in systems of belief, in mores and customs, in the way objects are used and physical life organized. It has to do with the way in which patterns of life in a group are structured with an emphasis on how these structures are experienced, understood and interpreted. These structures and their meanings influence the ongoing collective experience of groups. They also, on the other hand, limit, modify and constrain how groups live and interpret their life experiences. Moreover, there is a historical interaction constantly taking place between people and their changing social environment and circumstances. Culture is therefore never static. Instead there is a continual interplay resulting in dynamism, adaptability, reinterpretation, reformulation and change. There is certainly continuity, but this is itself continually challenged by changing circumstances. As such, new forms of expression, new perceptions and creative inter-pretations are emerging all the time. It is also important to point out that membership of a particular social group does not imply endorsement of every aspect of the group's culture. There are significant individual differences within each social group. This also is an important social reality.

An intercultural study attempts to capture the complexity involved in the interactions between people who have been and are being shaped and influenced by different cultures. It takes seriously the different expressions originating in different cultures but then proceeds by attempting to make possible a multi-perspectival examination of whatever issue is at stake. It recognizes that it is impossible to capture the totality of any given social group's culture. It realizes also that dominant or powerful groups may deliberately or unwittingly seek to impose their culture and perspective upon all others, or else control and select what is to be allowed expression. Worse still, and yet most common, has been the attempt to universalize and 'normalize' a particular culture's experience and judge all others by that one's views. This has been the case most clearly in the Eurocentric enterprise that has fuelled centuries of modernity. Such hegemonic attempts were pursued quite overtly in the period of Western expansionism, but even now often continue in subtle ways.

The way an intercultural approach seeks to counter such developments and to enhance interaction, therefore, is by giving many voices from different backgrounds a chance to express their views on the subject under review on their own terms. It does not then rush to analyze or systematize them into overarching theories that can explain and fit everything neatly into place. Instead, it ponders the glorious variety and chaotic mystery of human experience for clues to a more adequate response to the exigencies of human life. Such an approach has recently been termed 'postmodern,' and more will be said about this in the following section.

An intercultural approach is opposed to *reductionism* and *stereotyping* in any form. It takes the view that stereotyping is a particularly neurotic form of reductionism, in which, as a result of an inability to cope with complexity or difference, an attempt is made to control by placing groups in hierarchical order, categorizing them and seeing any particular individual member of a particular group as bearing the presumed characteristics of that group. Some well-meaning attempts to inform counselors and other carers about 'ethnic minority clients' adopted in many forms of 'multicultural training,' fall into this trap by perpetuating the myths, for example, about the angry underachieving Caribbean male; the Asian young woman's oppressive cultural role; the African student's problem with communication; the problems of the Asian extended family or the single-parent Caribbean family. As such, far from enabling attention to the particular client in question, these forms fuel stereotyping of the most heinous kind.

On the contrary, interculturality values *diversity* most highly. In an intercultural approach, culture's influence on belief and behavior is taken very seriously, without it being seen as determining them, or as the sole factor to be explored in examining them.

Interculturality is a creative response to the pluralism that is a fact of life in present-day society. It calls for the affirmation of three basic principles: *contexuality, multiple perspectives* and *authentic participation.*

The principle of contexuality asserts that every piece of behavior and every belief must be considered in the framework within which it takes place. It is within this framework of surrounding beliefs and worldviews that its meaning and significance can be gauged. Whereas context does not determine behavior or belief, it has a highly significant influence upon them. Behavior or belief are thus rendered meaningless or inexplicable without some attention to context. Pastoral caregivers in particular need to take social, cultural, economic, political and environmental contexts seriously, in view of their influence upon people's life experience and the interpretations they make of it.

The principle of multiple perspectives realizes that equally rational persons can examine the same issue and yet arrive at very different understandings. It goes on to insist that these different perspectives need to be seen as equally deserving of attention. Through a process of listening and dialogue, one or other, or combinations of these perspectives, may prove more adequate in coping with a particular issue in a given context. Monocausal explanations of phenomena – especially personal and social experience – are usually inadequate and can actually prove oppressive. The view that there is one total explanation of any experience is considered untruthful in intercultural pastoral care. Power dynamics are seen to be at play in interpretations and explanations of human experience. Total and complete explanations have usually been handed down by the powerful to the powerless in situations.

The principle of authentic participation is premised upon mutual concern for the integrity of the 'other,' and affirms the right of all to participate in discussion and examination of an issue on their own terms, realizing that there are strengths and weaknesses in every approach. Interculturalists seek to encourage diversity through making space for 'the others' to participate. This participation is not seen as permitted by a 'tolerant' powerbroker, but rather as a theological imperative of creation.

Augsburger (1986) has argued, quite rightly, that one needs more than just information about another culture to become culturally aware. 'This change,' he argues, 'comes from encounter, contact and interaction, not from programmic education or social engineering. It occurs on the boundary, not in the cultural enclave' (p.25). For cross-cultural counseling it is necessary to be aware not simply of superficial, visibly different cultural traits, but also of significant and subtle issues of similarity and difference between people. Indeed it calls for an awareness of meaning within a different set of values and beliefs together with an ability to 'think and feel' the difference. As Augsburger puts it:

> The capacity not only to 'believe' the second culture but to come to understand it both cognitively ('thinking with') and affectively ('feeling with') is necessary before one enters cross-cultural counselling. (p.26)

Interculturality affirms a 'Trinitarian' formulation of human personhood expressed by Kluckholn and Murray as far back as 1948.[2] Each assertion of the threefold statement is true and important in itself. Each needs to be held in relation to the others within a unity that holds together and transcends opposites.

Every human person is in certain respects:

1. LIKE ALL OTHERS

2. LIKE SOME OTHERS

3. LIKE NO OTHER.

In the first assertion, testimony is borne to characteristics that all human persons have in common. We are all born helpless, grow from dependence toward relative self-management, we relate to other beings and to a physical environment and ten out of ten die! In this sense, all humans share characteristics that make us distinctly human.

The second assertion recognizes that precisely because we are human we are each shaped, influenced and patterned to some extent by the community within which we are socialized. This matrix of values, beliefs, customs and basic life assumptions which we call culture, as we have previously indicated, is shared to a large extent, with those who share or have shared the community's life and socializing influences.

The third points to the uniqueness of each individual. Each person has a unique genetic code, voice pattern, fingerprint and dental configuration. Each person has a distinct life story, developmental history and particular lifestyle. No other person will ever see, think, feel, celebrate or suffer in an identical way.

It is dangerous to overemphasize any one of these to the exclusion of the others. On the other hand, in order to gain a fuller understanding of human persons, it is necessary to explore the 'unique and simultaneous influences of cultural specificity, individual uniqueness and human universality' (Speight 1991, p.11).

Many attempts at multicultural or cross-cultural training have focused almost exclusively on the cultural aspect, often producing lists of culturally specific characteristics to be studied by Westerners to equip them to respond to 'specific minority cultures.' Such attempts often grossly overemphasize cultural phenomena. Where the wrong-headedness of this approach has been recognized, the proposed solution for the problem has been to suggest an emphasis on existential or human universals (see Fukuyama 1990; Vontress 1985). However, in the long run such an emphasis is also inadequate precisely because it does not take culture or individual uniqueness seriously enough. Draguns (1989) wrestles with the dilemma of the universal versus the culturally distinctive and concludes that 'the best approach is somewhere in between, even though we do not yet know exactly where' (p.14).

The most illuminating approach appears to me to be what I am calling interculturality. Here the complex interrelatedness and interconnectedness of the three spheres interacting in living, growing and changing human persons is what is expected, treated as the norm and attended to. Interculturality, therefore, while at various points in a discussion may focus on one or other of these aspects of our humanity, seeks always to have the others in view and therefore to hold all three in creative and dynamic tension.

Augsburger's (1986) cross-cultural counseling, is an attempt to be 'at home on the boundary' to have the capacity to enter creatively into each 'culture' and thus to function as one who mediates and reconciles. In spite of its clear strengths, even this approach is unable to escape the dangers of cultural stereotyping and the fostering of a 'them and us' mentality. Interculturality, alternatively, speaks of *living in the intersection* of the three spheres – being centered in the intersection of the universal, the cultural and the individual within living, colourful persons. It is *inter* cultural precisely because it emphasizes interaction between and among many persons, groups and perspectives.

An intercultural approach to pastoral care and counseling, therefore, raises three kinds of questions of the persons and situations it encounters. Research based on this approach has to seek to respond to these three levels of experience and spheres of influence.

- *What of the universal experience of humanity is to be found here?* To what extent is a particular experience common to all human beings? The forms of expression and configuration of the experience may differ, but what is universal about the core experience?

- *What is culturally determined about this way of thinking, feeling or behaving?* The task here is to attempt to figure out what in the experience being confronted is a function of social and cultural forces. Examples of these would include the influence of child-raising practices, socialization, gender and role expectations, and the processes and ideologies of racialization.[3]

- *What in this experience can be said to be uniquely attributable to this particular person?* Here, the practitioner needs to seek the differences that are due to individual particularities shining through the person's experience.

These three are explored more fully as pastoral questions in the final chapter of this work.

A book written from an intercultural perspective may be presented in at least two ways. The first is as an edited collection with different people writing different chapters. A second is where one author presents material from a wide range of sources and viewpoints, attempting to make a fair presentation of different views on the material under consideration. Both approaches have obvious strengths and weaknesses. I have chosen to adopt the second approach, which offers the opportunity for me to attempt to *live in the intersection*, with the clear knowledge that culture, humanity and individual difference influence us all in ways which result in our finding similarity and difference in the most unexpected places. As such, although I am the author, several individuals and groups have made significant contributions to my thinking on the subjects covered. I have attempted to be respectful of them all. Most significant have been groups of students drawn from very many countries on the postgraduate diploma and MA courses in pastoral studies at the University of Birmingham, whom it has been my privilege to teach over many years. Although it is now very much a cliché to say this, it is true that I have learnt a great deal from our interactions – which have been cast in *living color*. I have found difference where ethnicity, race, class and gender might have suggested otherwise. I have also found similarity where every possible cultural indicator might have pointed in the opposite direction. We have wrestled on various topics with the universal, the cultural and the individual in each of us. I am obviously individually responsible for the errors and misunderstandings that are universally an inevitable part of such a cultural undertaking.

Postmodernism and postcolonialism

Since World War II, two major pillars of modernity, namely the sacredness of science and the inevitability of human progress, have been severely shaken. The mood of thought that has emerged since then, but especially since the 1960s, has been described as postmodern. This 'profound shift in the structure of feeling' (quoted by Harvey 1992, p.300), is present in a wide range of disciplines and cultural practices. It has been characterized in a variety of ways as an emergent culture, style, way or form of thinking.

Woods (1999), in a useful introductory text, describes postmodernism as representing 'a decline of faith in the keystones of the Enlightenment – belief in the infinite progress of knowledge, belief in infinite moral and social advancement, belief in teleology – and its rigorous definition of the standards of intelligibility, coherence and legitimacy' (p.11). Postmodernism entails a critique, or in more virulent forms rejection, of modernism and its Enlightenment garb. In Jean-François Lyotard's famous phrase, it is an 'incredulity towards metanarratives' and a challenge to all totalizing discourses. This disillusionment with ambitious 'total explanations' of reality such as offered by science, religion or grand political schemes like

Marxism, has ushered in an era where micronarratives (i.e. smaller-scale local, personal, or single-issue stories) are more highly valued than before. Provisional, rather than universal and absolute forms of legitimation are sought.

Postmodernism espouses views born out of a realization that knowledge can only ever be partial, fragmented and incomplete, and as such there is an anti-foundationalism that challenges and rejects the claims of universal organized bodies of knowledge that present themselves as mediating 'neutral', disinterested truth. In place of these, knowledge is seen as located and contextual. The social, economic, cultural and political location of persons significantly affects their apprehensions and inter-pretations of phenomena. The suppression of knowledge by powerful and privileged groups is a matter of investigation and interest to post-modernists.

One of the hallmarks of postmodernism has been a fascination with alterity (otherness). The 'other' who is significantly different from the self (i.e. the Western self) is to be highly valued, listened to and learned from. This is because multiple positions and perspectives are seen as highly significant and pluralities of discourse that recognize diverse truths and divergent histories, are prized. Different forms of knowledge that have been subjugated are given the opportunity to be released, find expression and be explored. It is instructive to note that peoples of what has been described in some circles as the 'Two Thirds' world, most of whom experienced imperialism, slavery, colonization and marginalization, have long been doubtful of the grand narratives of the West. Many have often sighed their objections to the veracity of the stories of the conquerors under their breaths. With the rise of movements for independence in many Western colonies came more overt expressions of incredulity together with calls for the voices of the oppressed to be heard. Postcolonial literature, political resistance movements, womens' movements and organizations under apartheid in South Africa, for example – which used names like 'football club' to mask their social, educational and political activities – have long struggled for the elevation of 'subjugated knowledge,' the overthrow of the grand narratives of the powerful and the democratization of education. These movements and peoples represent a postmodernism of the oppressed.

Instead of a presumed homogeneity, it is the complexities and contradictions inherent in heterogeneity that are celebrated. As such heterogeneity and difference are privileged. Moreover, sharp binary oppositions between say, science and literature, fact and fiction, reason and intuition, or high art and popular art, are challenged. The crucial question here is that of power – especially the power to define or categorize. Postmodernism is skeptical about the assumed 'right' of some to define what is to be described as 'high,' 'cultured' or important to the neglect and often detriment of others. Jacques Derrida's (1976) theories of deconstruction and grammatology have particularly sought to disrupt the illusions of privilege and priority surrounding the preferred term in these and other binary oppositions.

Michel Foucault is perhaps the postmodern thinker who has done most to analyze power both in its macro as well as micro dynamics. Foucault helps us realize just how pervasive power struggles are. He also makes us see that struggles of resistance are intertwined with all exercising of power.

Emphasis in postmodernism, is laid upon the social construction of identities in opposition to the essentialism that seeks to locate identity in a physiological or cultural essence uniting all who share it. Identity is seen as fluid and multiple, reflecting the trajectories of social exposure that persons have followed. In the pursuit of social constructionism of identity, and indeed the challenge of foundationalism and metanarratives, postmodernism tends to encourage interdisciplinarity. It is as the various disciplines, whose boundaries and subject matter are in any case questioned by postmodernists, dialogue with each other that something approximating reality can be reached for.

The postmodern condition into which we have been ushered is characterized on the one hand by ephemerality and uncertainty – a situation that has been sharply criticized by many – and on the other hand by endless possibilities for new ways of being. There clearly is much in postmodernism that is in line with the underlying philosophy of intercultural pastoral care. *In Living Color* enters into the creativity of the new way opened up by postmodernist thought, inspired largely by the movement that arose in certain quarters long before postmodernism, and in others contemporaneously with it, and that has been described as *postcolonialism*.

Postcolonialism and postmodernism share many features. Amidst the plethora and productivity of postcolonial literature and discourse, R.S. Sugirtharajah's work is most illuminating. Sugirtharajah (2002) argues that postcolonialism was not originally conceived of as a new theory; instead it comprised 'creative literature as resistance discourse emerging in the former colonies of the Western empires' (p.11). Chinua Achebe's novel *Things Fall Apart* (1965), which described and analyzed the effects upon Nigerian traditional society of the arrival and activities of European colonialists, is a powerful piece of historical fiction that ushered in postcolonial African literature. Indeed 'postcolonial studies emerged as a way of engaging with the textual, historical, and cultural articulations of societies disturbed and transformed by the historical reality of colonial presence' (Sugirtharajah 2002, p.11).

Homi Bhabha (1994) writes, 'postcolonial criticism bears witness to the unequal and uneven forces of cultural representation involved in the contest for political and social authority within the modern world order' (p.171). Sugirtharajah demonstrates its simultaneous emergence as a style of inquiry in a range of disciplines, notably English, anthropology, geography, international studies and history. He shows how the text that paved the way for postcolonial criticism's internal academic reform, namely Edward Said's *Orientalism* published in 1978, was able to establish the connection between the production of academic knowledge and colonialism. Knowledge is power and he who held and shaped knowledge was the ruler, knowing better than the ruled (whose knowledge was discounted, subjugated or ridiculed). Postcolonial criticism contests and subverts this established pattern, challenges the nature of the knowledge of the colonizer and turns attention to the nature of subjugated knowledge. Rather than engaging in fruitless contestations as to which came first, postmodernism or postcolonialism, it is more useful to appreciate the irruption of subjugated knowledge embodied by both modes of thought and to attempt to see how they may help us to realize the rich and complex diversity within the created order.

In Living Color recognizes that the global situation is one in which the pre-colonial, colonial, neo-colonial and postcolonial co-exist. Similarly the pre-modern, modern and postmodern are present simultaneously in many places. The global reality is complex and diffuse. Whilst some discourse within a postmodern climate, others live in pre-modern conditions. Often these exist within the same locality. For many, the technological trappings of postmodernity sit alongside pre-modern cultural assumptions, neo-colonial political forces, postcolonial resistance struggles through art and music, and postmodernist frustration with globalized discourse. It is within this complexity that pastoral practitioners live. Pastoral caregivers cannot practice their art as if in an isolated time warp. Social and cultural forces impinge upon the practice of pastoral care and counseling. Pastoral caregivers need to engage in social and cultural analysis in the midst of the changing times. There is a need to hold cultural and socio-economic conditions together if our considerations are to address the needs of a global and globalizing world.

The tragic and horrendous events of September 11th 2001 in the US, continue to have an impact on, and reverberate round, the world. They emphasize the need for increased intercultural dialogue. The global village has been on fire for centuries, and as Archbishop Rowan Williams (2002, p.53) puts it, 'in the global village, fire can jump more easily from roof to roof.' *In Living Color* is written to facilitate our global interaction in the light of the fire, and to help us all replace fire with understanding.

Notes

1. For a concise and useful introduction to various usage of the term, see Hall and Gieben (1992, pp.229–237).

2. This is presented and discussed helpfully in Augsburger (1986, pp.48–78).

3. For a recent useful discussion of 'racialization' see Small 1994, especially pp.29–39.

CHAPTER 2

Historical Developments
in Pastoral Care

Pastoral care as we have it today is in certain important respects, a contemporary expression of the age-long activity or ministry of the 'cure of souls' (*cura animarum*) offered throughout the centuries by various religious persons, philosophers, sages and communities of different kinds. John McNeill explores this activity from the earliest times beginning with the sages of ancient Semitic cultures in a book entitled *A History of the Cure of Souls* (1977). Egypt and Babylon had classes of dispensers of guidance, and in fact Egyptian works of this kind are among the earliest extant writings of humanity. In this regard, reference could be made to the Egyptian 'Teaching of Kagemma', the 'Wisdom of Ptah-hotep', or the 'Teaching of Amen-em-ope.' The writing of Ptah-hotep, 2800 years before Christ, is replete with moral injunction including appeals for the avoidance of arrogance, conceit and covetousness in line with 'the weighty sayings of the ancestors' (McNeill 1977, p.3). The *Maxims of Ahikar* believed to be a work of about 500 BCE, which appeared in Aramaic, Syriac, Armenian and Arabic are a particularly vivid example of the stories-with-a-moral which have come to us from the Babylonians and other peoples of the Euphrates region.

In Israel, the sages appear to have had a much lower profile than the more visible prophets. The names of four early Israelite sages are preserved for us in 1 Kings 4:31 (and 1 Chronicles 2:6) where their wisdom is compared with that of Solomon: 'Solomon was wiser than all men, than Ethan the Ezrahite, and Heman, and Calcol and Darda, sons of Mahol.' Jewish Wisdom writers, influenced to an extent by Greek sages, produced works like the books of Ecclesiastes, Ecclesiasticus and The Wisdom of Solomon. These writings present collections of the sayings of the sages who offered practical guidance for daily living. They are cast in an educational mode and use reasoned argument to offer the accumulated wisdom of 'grey beards' seeking to mould the lives of the young and the morally immature.

Socrates, we are told, wished to be known as *iatros tes psuches* (healer of souls). His overarching influence upon Plato, Xenophon and later philosophers, notably the Academicians and the Stoics, is well known and is also in evidence in the works of Cicero and Plutarch. The notion of the philosopher's function as physician of the soul was given renewed expression by many. Perhaps the greatest expression of this function was in the development of the consolatory essay, typically written to bring comfort to the bereaved. While Cicero's views of *iatroi logoi* (healing words) for the bereaved would seem today to be quite inappropriate, it is interesting to observe the care and attention paid to death, sorrow and suffering, and the serious efforts to enable people to overcome these through reasoned discourse appropriately adapted to the particular circumstances. On the other hand, the Academician Crantor's opposition to the Stoic demand for *apatheia* and his appeal for emotional release of grief, though in moderation, would seem to be very modern in terms of current views on the importance of grieving. Socrates, then, was 'a great forerunner of the many who have searched out and sifted the thoughts of men for the healing and well-being of their souls.' (McNeill 1977, p.41).

The religious faiths of the continent of Asia have historically offered care for people in different ways. Western writers seeking to explain the 'cure of souls' in Eastern contexts have pointed to the tradition of mentoring found in almost all Eastern religious faiths. In Hindu practice the different classes of *guru* (revered counselor and guide); in Islam the *murshid* (one who guides), the *pir* or else the *sheik* (old man) have been offered as Eastern versions of the spiritual director in Roman Catholic practice or the priest in general Western religious traditions. It seems to me that much is to be learnt from the nature and teaching of these persons on their own terms and with an understanding of the contexts within which the practice was set, if one is to avoid misunderstanding or inappropriate comparison. It is necessary to explore the different types of relationship on offer in Hinduism, Zen Buddhism and Islam, for example, in order, on the one hand, not to overvalue them and subject them to an inappropriate Western cultural analysis or, on the other hand, grossly to undervalue them, with the result that the nature of the relationship between guide and follower is misunderstood.

In line with an intercultural approach an attempt is made to recognize the significance of faith stances for pastoral care. However, much more emic (from within the various faiths) expression than is possible here is needed for the difference and complexity of each tradition in the different social and national contexts to be truly heard on their own terms.

Clebsch and Jaekle (1967) restrict themselves to a study of pastoral care in the Christian era. They are convinced on the basis of their study, of two characteristic historic features of Christian pastoral care, namely creativity and contextuality. Christian pastoral care has been exercised in a great variety of ways and with a great deal of ingenuity. Each act of Christian pastoral care, nonetheless, stands within and draws upon a specific human, historical, cultural and ecclesial context. In apparent response to the criticism that practitioners of pastoral care in the modern period have leant too heavily on the discipline of psychology, Clebsch and Jaekle are sure that Christians have always made use of available material from the current human and social sciences, suitably adjusted or adapted, in their pastoral caring.

Clebsch and Jaekle see four basic functions of Christian pastoral care – healing, guiding, sustaining and reconciling – all operating down through the years, with one particular function being dominant in a specific time period in response to historical circumstance. They divide Christian history into eight periods and provide exhibits to illustrate the thesis that a particular function predominates in each one. So, for example the period of the persecutions of Christians (ca 180–306 CE) is characterized by the function of reconciling as Christians were prompted by official threats to renounce their faith and swear allegiance to the Emperor. Pastoral care took the form of reconciling apostates to the Church, reconciling faithful believers to the once lapsed, and bringing factions within the church together again.

All this changed with Constantine's accession to power in 312. With Christians in a favourable position and Christianity now seen as the great unifier of society, pastors now find that they are called upon to provide guidance for perplexed persons as to how to conduct their affairs. Pastors have to show how various social activities have both cultural significance and Christian meaning. They at this time sought to interpret the problems and difficulties people faced in Christian terms so as to be able to offer responses compatible with the faith while also in keeping with knowledge and culture.

Useful as Clebsch and Jaekle's broad sweep approach is in giving an overview of Christian pastoral care, it can be, and has been, criticized on historiographical grounds. Culbertson and Shippee (1990) make this criticism and show how much more work is needed on pastoring in specific periods of Christian history. They focus on the Patristic period and show the diversity of issues and approaches even in that limited time frame. Oden (1984), for different reasons, focuses on Pope Gregory the Great (540–604) for careful study, as an example of the tremendous value of classical Christian pastoral care for this day and age.

Some early examples

Pope Gregory's *Liber Regulae Pastoralis* has been described as the most widely read single text in the history of pastoral care. Gregory wrote this essay to his friend John, Archbishop of Ravenna, to explain his very great reluctance to take up the papal office in 590. The work is in four parts: the first explaining the immense difficulty of the pastoral office and the requirements it places on those called to it; the second setting forth the inner and outer life of the good pastor; the third a fascinating collection of different ways to respond pastorally to a very wide range of differing 'sorts and conditions' of human persons including 'the young and the old, the impudent and the timid, the hale and the sick...sowers of discord and peacemakers...those who commit only small sins but commit them frequently, and those who guard themselves against small sins yet sometimes sink into grave ones' (Gregory the Great 1950, pp.90–92). The final section implores the pastor to be self-critical.

Among the many striking and relevant issues a reader of Gregory's work may notice is, on the one hand, the personal humility required of the one taking up pastoral care and, on the other, the grand and honourable position that such a person is deemed to have entered upon. The very obvious place spirituality occupies in the conception of pastoral care proposed, shines through together with the serious, if rather moralistic attempt, to deal with specific issues and the particular circumstances of each person cared for.

Davis, in the introduction to his translation of Pope Gregory's work, quotes Dudden with approval when Dudden declares: 'Its [the book's] influence during this period can scarcely be overrated – indeed, it is felt even now in its results. The maxims of Gregory have moulded the Church' (Gregory the Great 1950, p.12).

Taking another hugely influential text from Christian history we turn to the Puritan divine Richard Baxter (1615–1691) who provided for English-speaking Christians the standard textbook in pastoral theology during the age of the Enlightenment. His book, *The Reformed Pastor*, first published in 1656, exerted tremendous influence upon generations of pastors. Baxter wrote at a time of great ministerial decline, and his principal objective was, by appeal and persuasion, to proclaim the primary value of the pastoral function of Christian ministry. He was convinced that Christian education was needed both through preaching and 'private conference from house to house.' Once again the spiritual nature of ministry is emphasized. In fact, in Baxter, the 'blessedness of the life to come, compared with the vanities of this present life,' is a constant theme.

We shall return to the theme of spirituality in a later chapter. Suffice it to say here that in Baxter, an emphasis on the hereafter did not mean a neglect of care and concern for people in their existential circumstances, rather it was the fuel that fired a ministry of visiting and that of expressing Christian love in people's homes.

Thomas Oden (1993) has pointed towards a 'great pastoral tradition' within Christianity, by reference to historical figures and texts from seven categories.

1. Early Christian psychology – for example Augustine's *The Greatness of the Soul* or Tertullian's *A Treatise on the Soul.*

2. The Pastoral Office – including Cyprian's *Letters and Treatises* and Chrysostom's *On Priesthood.*

3. Pastoral Counseling – for example Bonaventura's *The Governance of the Soul.*

4. Pastoral Instructions – including *Parochalia* by Bishop Thomas Wilson and the letters of Ambrose.

5. Models of the Working Pastor – for example Luther's *Letters of Spiritual Counsel* or *Country Parson* by George Herbert.

6. The Caring Community – including *Rules of Bonds* by John Wesley and the *Institutes* of John Cassian.

7. Pastoral Theology – for example Schleiermacher's *Die Praktische Theologie* or *Théologie Pastorale ou Théorie du Ministère Évangélique* by Alexandre Vinet.

(adapted from Oden 1993, pp 66–67)

Oden expresses the concern that these and other texts need to be restudied and re-appropriated as classical theological and pastoral resources for pastoral care today. Although this is not the place to embark on such a study, Oden's call seems to me welcome since it entails studying pastoral care within historically and culturally different societies. Such study is itself intercultural because it involves imaginative, interpathic entry into historically distant cultures with respect, in order to listen to the wisdom contained therein. Hermeneutical questions concerning the use of the findings of such studies contemporaneously need to be posed, though, as also issues of the significance of appeals to the 'good old days' and the reductionism which fails to see the presence of transcendence in any but past times.

An Islamic exemplar

Although there is clearly a largely communitarian and unitarian sense in Islamic teaching and guidance, it is important to remember that as a result of geographical and contextual differences, different schools (*madhab*) grew up in different centres. As Islam spread in the early centuries it appears that here and there individuals were drawn to more personal responses to the divine unitive mystery heralded by the Prophet Mohammed. By the tenth century Sufi Orders (*tariqat*) had developed around well-respected Sufis. Most prominently in India, perhaps encouraged by the Hindu tradition of the guru-chëlä relationship, outstanding Sufis attracted followers. One such renowned Indian Sufi spiritual leader was Sharafuddin Ahmad ibn Yahya Maneri (1290–1381). Son of his father Yahya, a well known Sufi in his times, and mother Bibi Razia, young Ahmad grew up to become known later as Makhdum ul-Mulk, 'The Spiritual Teacher of the Realm.' To this day, people in his birth place Maner, and throughout the north-east Indian state of Bihar, refer to him as *Makhdum Sahib* and annually commemorate the anniversary of his death, as is customary among Sufis. Syed Hasan Askari (1980) writes:

> Many Sufi orders came to Bihar – the Chisti, the Shattari, the Qadiri and the Naqshbandi. But Makhdum al-Mulk Sharafuddin b. Yahya Maneri eclipsed the leaders of all these orders. He still enjoys immense popularity in religious and official circles among Hindus as well as Muslims, a tribute that has been denied to other medieval Sufi masters and that explains the popularity of the order he introduced to Bihar, the Firdausiya. (p.*xii*)

Sharafuddin studied first at his local mosque-school and later accompanied Abu Tawwama, a noted scholar from Delhi to Sonargoan, in modern-day Bangladesh, where he received a standard and thorough Islamic education. After his father's death, Sharafuddin left for Delhi, in search of spiritual guidance. He met with Sheik Nizamuddin Auliya and later with Sheik Bu Calendar of Pinniped, both in the very last years of their lives and both unable to offer him any real guidance. It was at the point of disappointment when, at the suggestion of his brother, he met with a less well-known Sufi, Sheik Najibuddin Firdausi. 'It was this meeting which changed his life and enabled him to become a great spiritual guide himself, for he was instantly attracted to Najibuddin and entrusted himself to his care and guidance' (Jackson 1990, p.193). On the death of Najibuddin eight years later, Sharafuddin set out to return home to Maner. Spending a year in the jungle of Bihia, he ended up in a cave in Rajgir. His desire for solitude was not fulfilled, for disciples of many Sheikhs came to seek guidance from him as well as many ordinary people wanting him to write letters of petition to local Muslim administrators on their behalf.

Sharafuddin did not seek to be a guide. Instead, he was sought out by people who found in him the light they sought. Among the legacies he has left to posterity are *The Hundred Letters*. These were written instructions he sent to Qazi Shamsuddin, governor of Chausa in western Bihar, at the Qazi's request, for his spiritual advancement. They were compiled by Zain Badr Arabi, who attended Sharafuddin. Letters 5, 6 and 7 address the quest for a spiritual guide, the qualifications of a Sheik and discipleship, respectively. Sharafuddin Maneri writes:

God guides whomsoever He wishes! (Q.42:52). Wherever that seed is found, some form of guidance, either through the role of a prophet or that of a sheik, the prophet's deputy, is necessary. (Jackson 1980, p.25)

He is as convinced of the necessity of a guide as he is of God's willingness to provide one for the earnest seeker.

You are an ant; the Way is like the long tresses of beauty.

Beware, O man, of merely guessing or blindly following others. (Jackson 1980, p.26)

In line with his own experience, he is convinced that it may be necessary to associate with 'two, three, four, or even more guides in order to reach the Goal.' But the novice must always be courteous about a particular guide's stage of development even when he has to leave him for further growth.

Of the sheik, Maneri says, 'he should be a man who has experienced both the horror of God's majesty and the delight of his beauty.' Since the disciple is required to be completely devoted to the guide, there are clear expectations of the character and qualification of the sheik. There are five stages to becoming a guide. The first is the submission common to all servants or disciples; the second is the disposition to receive truths from God directly without an intermediary; the third is divinely inspired submission specially given; the fourth is the honor of actually receiving direct divine knowledge; and the fifth, the riches that such reception bestows. Clearly, humility evidenced in submission, coupled with divine grace and knowledge are the prerequisites for leadership here.

There are many inspiring passages in Sharafuddin Maneri's work that would be of value to any pastoral practitioner in the quest for guidance. It is the case that Sufis – both men and women – have been of immense value in pointing many in useful directions in their desire for illumination.

Some more recent developments

Pastoral care has continued to attract varied responses and signs of interest through the years and in different settings. Among the more significant recent developments has been the coming together into an international movement of reflective practitioners of pastoral care and counseling from several different countries across the world. The first such gathering was held in Edinburgh, Scotland, from the 8th to the 15th of August, 1979 with the theme 'The risks of freedom.' This congress was attended by over four hundred people from all continents and evoked memories, expressed by the Moderator of the General Assembly of the Church of Scotland, of the crucial ecumenical meetings of 1910 and 1937 in Edinburgh (See the publication of the papers of this congress: Becher, Campbell and Parker, 1993.) It is striking that at this very first world congress voices were heard not only from Europe and the US but also from Africa and Asia. However, the congress began to face the complex issues of communication, learning, method and culture within the bewildering varieties of nationality, religious denomination, modes of presentation and of approach to pastoral care. Alistair Campbell captured the challenge for the fledgling movement for pastoral care and counseling in these words:

> There is the challenge to the cultural captivity of pastoral care, which was posed by the richness of the Edinburgh experience. It is no longer possible to speak comfortably of care, whilst ignoring the political, social and economic oppressions of our world; no longer permissible to assume that one culture – in West or East, in North or South – can supply all the insights needed to restore humanity to man; no longer valid to speak of freedom without recognising its complexity and without acknowledging the risks entailed in truly seeking it for all men and women. (Becher *et al.* 1993, p.147)

In a profound sense, the issues raised at this first congress seem to have set the tone for and expressed the concerns that practitioners of pastoral care and counseling have continued to grapple with in and outside congresses since 1979.

The second international congress was held in San Francisco in August 1983 on the theme 'Symbols and stories in pastoral care and counseling.' In a sense, this gathering served as a 'home-coming' for many participants whose training had either been within the US, in clinical pastoral education, or else in models and approaches originating in the US. Fewer formal papers were presented at this congress. Instead, as David Lyall, writes 'participants from four continents dramatically portrayed something of their history and culture as a context for pastoral care' (Becher *et al.* 1993, p.9). From Europe, the issue of the enormous differences of language, culture and religion, which have so often torn Europe apart, were presented. From Africa, the reality of warmth and love in the midst of appalling deprivation and clash of cultures. From Asia, a realization that 'organising people into continents is even more destructive than herding them into smaller national or religious groups' (Foskett 1984, p.25). The Asians conveyed in their stories the ways in which the poor make use of clinical pastoral education. From North America came a moving presentation in which the fractures of American history and society in relation to the 'victims' of the American Dream shone through.

The theme of the third congress held in Melbourne, Australia in August 1987 building on San Francisco, was 'Pastoral ministry in a fractured world.' The format of this meeting combined the formal papers – two speakers on each topic – with theme groups made up of roughly twenty participants selected to be a representative cross-section of the nations and cultures present in the congress. The four topics addressed were, culture, person-in-community, movement toward sexual equality, and the oppressed and the oppressor. Presenters sought pastoral responses to each of these issues. The highpoint of the congress occurred on the final day when Carolee Chanona and Jose Marins from South America made a presentation on the pastoral response to the oppressed and the oppressor. The two are an itinerant pastoral team that emerged in response to the Bishops' Conference of Medellin in 1968, the conference that saw the formal birth of Latin American Liberation Theology. This is how they began:

> We will speak to you from the special vantage point of the Basic Ecclesial Communities as they grapple with this challenge and seek to respond pastorally to the situation of oppression. Our presentation will in part be using the language of our people who at the grass-roots level are classified as illiterate and who thus have recourse to the language of symbols. We will allow them to speak of and to their realities as experienced in their day-to-day living and then reflect with you upon the theological implications and pastoral challenges of this reality in our part of the world. (ICPCC 1987, p.94)

Behind the speakers were banners, paintings, pictures and icons from Panama, Bolivia, Haiti, Brazil and the Dominican Republic. John Foskett (1988) writes: 'For once words fell into place as a simple commentary on the message borne across oceans of space and experience, and yet immediately striking chords within us' (p.9). The congress stood to acclaim this presentation, which had taken participants through the now classic stages of experience to observation to reflection, and thence to understanding and action.

'Pastoral care and context' – so read the theme of the fourth international congress held in Noordwijkerhout, The Netherlands, in August 1991. Among the main presenters at this meeting were Jewish Rabbi and family therapist Edwin Friedman; Chilean psychiatrist and ordained minister Jorge Cardenas Brito; Padmasani Gallup, an Indian woman Professor in Social Ethics and Wilhelmina Kalu, family and child therapist and Senior Lecturer in Education at the University of Nigeria, Nsukka. Once again, there were small group and process group discussions where participants attempted to wrestle with the realities of their individual contexts against a background of the situations of others. One of the results of these discussions was the sense that the 'Third World' participants were still, by virtue of the inequalities of the global economic scene, largely marginalized and treated as guests, rather than as full participants at the congresses. In Holland a strong call was made for a congress to be hosted and held in the Third World. A clear struggle was emerging between those who insisted that the function of pastoral counseling was very different from social work or political action, and those whose view was that pastoral counseling could not be seriously practiced in a social and cultural vacuum.

The fifth congress was held in Toronto in August 1995. The rather unusual theme – 'Babylon and Jerusalem: Stories for transition in a strange land' – was a deliberate invitation 'to pursue themes which, in important ways, are different from those of previous meetings... We are being invited to consider or re-consider a much more universally inclusive understanding of pastoral care and counselling.' (from the First Announcement brochure of the congress). The main presentations at this meeting were offered from within different religious traditions. Rabbi Dow Marmur addressed the congress from a Jewish perspective, Elder Edna Manitowabi spoke out of her experience as a member of the Anishinabe (Ojibway) native Canadian nation and Faud Sahin, a Muslim medical practitioner spoke from an Islamic point of view. Suwanda Sugunasiri, a lecturer in education at the University of Toronto, offered Buddhist reflections. The Christian presentation was the very last and was offered by Alyson Barnett-Cowan, an Anglican priest and Ecumenical Officer of the Anglican Church of Canada.

The response to this courageous program was very mixed. Part of the negativity seemed to stem from the expectations of participants that speakers would make much use of 'stories' from their own traditions – an expectation which was not fulfilled, except to an extent in Rabbi Marmur's presentation. Another factor was the apparent gap between what the presenters offered and the practice of pastoral care and counseling as engaged in by the vast majority of participants. Nevertheless, it is significant that this congress sought to propel the movement on into the reality of pluralism in the religious and cultural contexts in which pastoral care and counseling is engaged in throughout the world today and to face pastoral practitioners with the ambiguities and difficulties in communication, and of learning, method and culture in the practice of pastoral care and counseling.

The sixth congress was held in Accra, Ghana, from the 8th to the 15th of August 1999, on the theme of 'Spirituality and culture in the practice of pastoral care and counselling.' This was the first to be held in a 'Third World' setting and to that extent fulfilled the dreams and aspirations of those who had called for such a gathering eight years before in Holland. The congress was perhaps the most diverse in terms of participation, with practitioners drawn from over 40 countries. The majority of the 175 participants, for the first time, came from African or Asian countries. Issues of contextualization, pluralization and globalization of pastoral care and counseling were very evident. Well-known African theologian John Mbiti, delivered a rousing and challenging keynote address entitled 'Aspects of healing practice in African independent churches and their contribution to pastoral care.' The four plenary presentations were offered by the following: Congolese professor Masamba ma Mpolo, illustrious doyen of African pastoral care and counseling, on 'The dynamics of symbols in African pastoral counselling'; Indian professor Nalini Arles of the United Theological College, Bangalore, drew on Dalit theology and spirituality to address the topic 'Spirituality and culture in the ministry of counselling'; Dr Ronaldo Sathler Rosa, Professor of Practical Theology at the Methodist University, Sao Paulo, Brazil, spoke on 'Pastoral action in a context of economic slavery and cultural apathy'; and Emefa Bonsi, a university campus counselor from Ghana, made a presentation on 'Cultural practices and church doctrine: Implications for pre-marital preparation and counseling in Ghana.' In very many respects, this congress represented a real step forward in the process of internationalization of the worldwide movement for pastoral care and counseling. For many, especially from the US and Europe, who made the journey to visit the slave castles at Elmina and Cape Coast, the conference itself and the opportunities it made possible, were unforgettable.

Important changes and developments are afoot within the disciplines of pastoral care and counseling as they are exposed to the experiences of ever-widening circles of people. National bodies such as the American Association of Pastoral Counselors (AAPC) and the Association for Clinical Pastoral Education (ACPE) are facing and addressing issues of cultural and ethnic diversity structurally as well as methodologically. Regional organizations for pastoral care and counseling exist in Africa, Asia-Pacific and Europe; and they too are deeply involved in the learning process captured well by Japanese priest and professor Takaaki David Ito in an address to the seventh Asia/Pacific Congress on Pastoral Care and Counselling held in Perth, Australia, in July 2001. Commenting on his trip to Ghana for the international congress in 1999, Canon Ito declared:

> The western model of spiritual care and therapy is not able to claim its universality any more. We learned that it was one's spiritual heritage that helped a person to be really her-/himself. One's self has been developed within a certain cultural setting as well as with her/his particular life history. As one can express one's thought most thoroughly with their mother tongue, one's spirituality flourishes most in one's culture. Because each of us grow in different cultures, fostered not only by its geography but also its history, it was really essential to listen to (the) voices of one's spirit always in relation to the cultural and historical background. It was the awareness of the importance of what is now called 'local knowledge'. Interestingly, local knowledge of a particular people may have significant relevance to therapy of another place and people. (Ito 2001, p.2)

Just as Takaaki Ito was inspired to go deeper into his own cultural and spiritual heritage for resources for his therapeutic work with the subjects of injustice in Japan through listening to the stories of Africans and others in an intercultural setting, so also many pastoral practitioners are reaping the fruits of such encounters for their own personal development and therapeutic practice.

CHAPTER 3

Models of Pastoral Care

In this chapter, five major models that manifest the shape and form of pastoral care will be examined. The assumptions underlying the approaches and the basic rationale for proceeding in each particular way will be explored. Setting them out in this way is not intended to imply mutual exclusivity or the absence of any degree of overlap in actual practice. Instead it is an attempt to assist in the necessary task of clarifying the assumptions and presuppositions upon which significant forms of pastoral care are based.

Pastoral care as therapy

The Greek word *therapeo*, from which the English word derives, essentially means 'to heal.' Healing presupposes that something has gone wrong with the proper functioning of bodies, minds or spirits. The fundamental understanding here then, is that some problem has arisen. Some malfunctioning has or is occurring in the smooth and proper running of things. This may be understood in medical terms as 'illness' or 'deviation from bio-physical norms' or else in theological terms as 'sin' or 'alienation from essence.'

Under this model, the task of the pastoral caregiver is to remove, or correct, what is wrong and in some way or by some means to return the sufferer to functioning order. Essentially the caregiver is there to make us better. The helper has a Messianic function. He or she heals, helps or saves us or enables us to be healed, helped or saved.

An assumption of this model is that it is possible to achieve the goals it seeks. So that by divine assistance, divine grace, or else some form of divine intervention, things can be made better. Where the divine is not invoked it is assumed that there are naturally occurring substances, or ways of behavior or thought, which are invested with the power to correct the malfunction. The caregiver's task is to discover these and to administer or recommend these to patients or clients. The strength of this model lies in the fact that it offers a clear and understandable 'problem' to which there is a 'solution.' It is premised upon first, diagnosing or recognizing what is wrong and then investing in a solution. Without an acknowledgment of a problem, no solution can be sought.

It has been argued that pastoral care in the latter part of the twentieth century has been in captivity to secular psychotherapy (see e.g. Oden 1984). The model that has seemed to be much in operation has been a therapeutic one. Pastoral care and especially pastoral counseling, has functioned largely, and effectively, as a form of psychotherapy. Moreover, it is also true to say that when pastoral care is modeled upon theologies of redemption (or 'soteriologies') which place great emphasis on the sinfulness of humanity, the greatness of the salvation wrought by the death of Christ and humanity's need for salvation, then pastoral care follows a therapeutic model and is subject to all the criticisms which such a view may be open to. These potential pitfalls include the danger of oversimplifying the issues at stake, the quest for single factors accountable for problems, the desire for quick-fix miracle cures, the problems of overdependence upon the curer or caregiver, and the potential for abuse by the powerful therapist.

Pastoral care as ministry

Where 'ministry' is the underlying assumption, pastoral care is understood as the operation or activity of particular persons, viewed as agents or intermediaries. Specific rites, procedures and training schemes are established for the recognition of those summoned by God to such activity and for their dedication to the task. Such persons function either individually or more usually in teams. They employ communication skills and sacramental rites to foster well-being, growth and spiritual advancement for groups such as communities of faith or individuals seeking spiritual direction.

Five classic activities are engaged in where pastoral care takes the form of ministry. Proclamation (*kerygma*) in which the essentials of belief and their attendant practices are set forth in coherent form for a community.

This includes the teaching (*didache*) and the prophecy (forth-telling) that form part of the round of activities in most communities of faith. Service (*diakonia*) often takes the form of particular deeds of kindness done for others. Almsgiving to the poor and needy, visiting and comforting the elderly and the sick, providing food and shelter for the homeless and destitute are some examples of pastoral care as service. An integral and historic part of such service, increasingly being recognized, concerns social and political action, about which more is said in the next section. Fellowship (*koinonia*) has to do with the provision of opportunities for social interaction within communities. Such communal activities include meals, games, celebrations and commemorations. Here the social nature of human existence is recognized and affirmed. Administration (*oikonomia*) is about the management and proper ordering of the institutional aspects of communal life. Financial affairs, property issues and legal matters need to be attended to if any organized social group, or individual for that matter, is to exist and function in a given society. Worship (*eucharistia*) offers the opportunity for communities of faith to express their spiritual longings and aspirations before God in meaningful and appropriate forms relevant to their beliefs and life experience. Most communities of faith would conceptualize worship as giving time, honor, space and recognition to God as the ultimate source of life. Worship is given to God within the context of social encounter as well as in private communion. In both cases, the object of worship is God. However, it is recognized that the love of God means that God cares for and engages with those who 'draw near to God.' The tasks of the leaders of worship include fashioning the structure of time and activity in such a way befitting and bespeaking the nature of God, so as to allow encounter with God whilst paying attention to the worshippers as people of differing phases of faith and psychosocial circumstance.

Pastoral care as social action

The rise of liberation theology in Latin America has had a marked influence on the way theology is studied and engaged in throughout the world. Latin American liberation theologians Leonardo and Clodovis Boff distinguish three levels of liberation theology – professional, pastoral and popular. Concerning pastoral liberation theology they write: 'It is the theology that sheds the light of the saving word on the reality of injustice so as to inspire the church to struggle for liberation' (Boff and Boff 1987, p.17). The model of pastoral care implied in this approach has been described as prophecy to structures or speaking truth to power. Essentially it is based on a socio-economic and political analysis of a specific social context. Such analysis is undergirded by historical criticism and theological reflection. Its aim is the transformation of societies and persons. The goal in view is a more socially just and equitable distribution of the human and material resources found on earth. Through participation in the life of the poor, an attempt is made to read the documents of faith and to examine the life situation from the perspective of the poor, the marginalized and the oppressed. Such an approach is from start to finish praxis (action-reflection) based. The Boff brothers point out that the Portuguese word for 'liberation', *liberação*, is composed of the root *liber* (free) and the Portuguese word for 'action' (*ação*). To transfer this coupling into English they coin the word libera(c)tion (Boff and Boff 1987, pp.4 and 10). This action-oriented, reflective process inspired by faith and commitment to the gospel is very much the shape and form pastoral care takes in many parts of the so-called Third World.

Pastoral care as empowerment

In contrast to a therapeutic model of pastoral care, in an empowerment model the emphasis is on the fact that there is something good, something of worth and value within human persons as they presently are. Empowerment implies not weakness but rather some pre-existing strength upon which one builds. The task of pastoral care under this model is the 'drawing out and building up' of the unnoticed strengths and resources within and around people and communities.

Empowerment models by and large, adopt educational and dialogical methods in facilitating the achievement of their goals. Inspired particularly by the works of Brazilian philosopher of education Paulo Freire (see especially Freire 1972a, 1972b), pastoral caregivers who work with an empowerment model seek to assist in the 'conscientization' of the oppressed and marginalized through enabling them to ask questions about their life situation. Conscientization is a process within which people become more aware of their situation and of the resources they possess to respond to and change things.

Pastoral care as personal interaction

In this model, relational skills are employed to assist people explore, clarify and change (or else cope more effectively with) unwanted thoughts, feelings and behavior. The focus tends to be on the individual, even when work is done in groups. In such interaction, much value is placed on the person cared for gaining insight. Insight is very often in terms of an interpretation of the matter causing concern along the lines of particular theories or schemes of understanding. As such, these approaches tend to be cognitive, using cause–effect theories which favor 'left-brain' logical, rational and analytical processes over 'right-brain' creative, intuitive, nonverbal processes.

Value is also placed upon verbal expressiveness, articulation of feelings and client self-disclosure within a warm, accepting and nonjudgmental environment largely produced by the carer's skills in personal relationship. Counseling is far and away a major example of this model and will be examined further in Chapter 5.

CHAPTER 4

Pastoral Care

Functions and Resources

Functions

What is pastoral care for? What purpose does it serve? Is there a need for it? Does it do any good? Can pastoral care be usefully distinguished from other forms of care? These and related questions go to the heart of the matter of pastoral care in the world today.

In many western European countries, the certainty and prominence that the role and function of pastor enjoyed in the past has been replaced by an uncertainty, insignificance, ambiguity and apparent redundancy. In many cases, the attraction offered by the clarity of professions such as counseling, social work, community work or management has been hard for pastors to resist. Where it has not been possible to change professions, the temptation has been to perform one's pastoral function with models, theories and practices borrowed from these professions. In other countries, notably in the so-called Third World as well as Eastern Europe and the US, pastoring is still very dearly valued, and pastors are invested sometimes with greater expectations than is warranted.

Questions about the functions of pastoring are contextual questions and demand contextual responses. In each cultural context, however, it is important that these questions be posed and adequate responses sought. Frank Wright, a Canon Emeritus of Manchester Cathedral, sought to respond within a British context in his book *The Pastoral Nature of the Ministry* (1980). He argues essentially that the pastor's task is to keep alive the mystery of God in the human situation. Wright quotes Cardinal Suhard, Archbishop of Paris in the late 1940s, to suggest that this means to 'so live one's life that it would be inexplicable if God did not exist' (Wright

1980, p.8). Wright argues that modern pastors, like artists, point to a reality beyond themselves, specifically 'the mystery of God.' It is this awareness of a transcendent reality, this conviction that the path to wholeness is not entirely of human endeavor, which is the pastor's task. 'It is sufficient, however, that that dimension is silently present, without any self-conscious references' (p.9). For David Deeks (1987), writing on 'the point of pastoral care,'

> Pastoral Theology begins with the search we all make for meaning in life. Pastoral theology takes with complete seriousness every struggle we engage in to understand ourselves, our culture, and the functioning of nature and society, and the connections between them. (p.67)

Deeks is convinced that the pastor(al theologian)

> is glad to be what we all are in reality: human beings grasping challenges and discoveries, exploring our personal identities, values and purposes, discovering our contexts in nature and history and puzzling over that mysterious relationship 'I' have with the world. (p.67)

Deeks's work very usefully sets out the starting point of what pastoring is about within a broad and inclusive framework. However, its strength is also at the same time its weakness. It is diffuse and frightfully overwhelming. Moreover, anyone engaged in any of the humanities could claim the same starting point.

Deeks becomes more specific in a chapter headed 'Pastoral care: Purpose and aims.' Here he writes very obviously from a Christian perspective, that the purpose of pastoral care is 'to assist men and women and boys and girls to live as disciples of Jesus' (p.80). He then offers and explores four aims. The first aim of pastoral care is to encourage people to make their own sense of their experience. The second is to disclose Christian meaning in life. Third, pastoral care aims to stimulate men and women to engage in their own conversation with the Christian tradition, and fourth, to encourage holiness (pp.80–94). By focusing on Christian thinking, Deeks helps us to see the implications in practice of the purpose of pastoral care in one specific tradition namely the Judaeo-Christian tradition which, it is true to say, has bequeathed the term 'pastoral care' to posterity.

The value of these writings is that they attempt to set forth in real terms the vision, motivation and aims that characterize pastoral care. They offer purpose and direction to pastoral caregivers. Thus they enable us to move from pastoral care as a series of practical 'hints and tips' to a consideration of purpose, a quest of underlying motivation and a sense of direction for activities many of which are shared with other 'caring' practitioners, such as social workers, community workers, nurses and therapeutic counselors.

There are four classic functions that pastoral care has been seen as serving. These are incorporated in the definition of pastoral care offered by Clebsch and Jaekle considered in Chapter 1. These are *healing, sustaining, guiding* and *reconciling*. To these, Clinebell has added a fifth, namely *nurturing*. In what follows we shall consider each of these functions in turn. But before we do that, I wish to suggest that there are at least two other functions that intercultural pastoral care and counseling clearly serves. In point of fact, the absence of these two invalidates much pastoral care in particular cultural contexts. These two are *liberating* and *empowering*. Let us then examine each of these functions in turn.

Healing

As human persons, we find ourselves broken and bruised in many ways. From time to time, we find ourselves in need of physical, emotional, psychological and spiritual restoration. Healing presupposes that we have lost something we once enjoyed and that it is possible to regain what we have lost. Often it is hoped that such restoration will take us further or place us in a better position than we were before. The art of healing entails those activities that facilitate the restoration sought for.

Healing is often thought about, certainly in a religious sense, in terms of 'miracles.' This way of thinking suggests an 'out of the ordinary' event, one that 'is inexplicable,' 'defies the laws of nature' or else is 'supernatural' in some sense. While not denying the possibility of such occurrences, medically referred to often as 'spontaneous remissions,' the way of thinking it exposes is often one in which a force, or power extrinsic to the world, 'intervenes' to change things in the world. Healers are then agents of this force. There are two points that need attention. First, the understanding of what is 'natural' is often in such cases very limited. It is necessary to examine what is understood as natural and what 'supernatural.' If one understands 'nature' to be far more complex than what meets the eye or what one can explain, then it becomes easier to see that what is termed miraculous could very well be 'natural.' Second, if we examine the meaning of intervention from an immanentist point of view, or one that sees the force or power of God as present in the world, it becomes possible to see God at work in and through the 'natural' processes in the world. In Christian thought, as also in African primal thinking, God is both transcendent and immanent. If this be so, then the task of healing, in pastoral terms, involves a recognition and a facilitation of the activity of the 'transcendent in the midst' of life. The God who heals is not one who is far away. Instead, such a God is present all the time and bears all the pain and anguish of the sufferer. But this God is also able and willing to help. The mystery is that we do not know God's intention or the form in which God's presence will take. This calls for openness and attentiveness.

The task of the pastoral healer then, is openness and attentiveness to the present. The pastoral healer listens deeply to the sighs and groans of humans in distress. The healer listens for, and is sensitive and open to, the transcendent in whatever form or shape, knowing that transcendence mediates love, support and help. Healers seek that their presence, words and activities become channels through which the love, support and help immanent in transcendence is mediated. By their openness, they respect the mystery and awesomeness of the divine. By their attentiveness, they may focus and direct themselves and the health-seekers to the presence of the divine that is so often in unexpected places.

Sustaining

In very many situations of life, healing, in the sense of restoration to a former position of strength or ability, simply does not or will not occur. To recognize and accept this is by no means easy. In fact, the struggle to survive, which often takes the form of the quest for healing through whatever means possible, seems to be an inbuilt tendency within humanity. It is this innate tendency that has sustained humanity in the face of disasters and tragedies that could have resulted in extinction. The massive growth of alternative therapies bears witness to humanity's amazing resilience and will-to-live. However, there comes a time when the realization that a situation is not going to get better dawns. The clearest example of this is in the event of death. When death has actually occurred, no amount of denial, natural as it is, is going to reverse it. It is in such circumstances that the art of sustaining is called for.

Sustaining goes beyond resignation. It is not about maintaining a stoic silence or a cynical resolution. To be sustained is to find strength and support, from within and without, to cope adequately with what cannot be changed. It has to do with a transformation of a situation by traversing through it, and is more to do with attitude than escape. Pastoral caregivers give support in such times not by promising a favorable outcome or better times, but by enabling and facilitating coping mechanisms within them. Or else by helping them draw upon sustaining forces outside themselves, within their immediate social or cultural circumstances.

Guiding

One of the features of life at the beginning of the twenty-first century is a bewildering variety of views on any subject under the sun. When confronted with any choice or decision in life the twenty-first century person may have recourse to many different philosophies of life, world-views, value systems, ideologies and perspectives. For many people, several options will for various reasons, be in practice out of their reach. However, even in those circumstances the contemplation of different options is possible. How is one to choose? How does one weigh the relative merits and demerits of any option? How is one enabled to examine and decide among the different possibilities? One crucial function of pastoral care is that of attempting to respond to these kinds of question.

The term 'guiding' has a paternalistic and archaic ring to it. In many contexts, the function it refers to is conveyed by current terms like 'problem-solving' or 'decision-making' skills. What it seems to me is required, especially from an intercultural perspective, is conveyed in the words of Islamic poet and philosopher, Kahlil Gibran:

> No man can reveal to you aught but that which already lies half asleep in the dawning of your knowledge.

> The teacher who walks in the shadow of the temple, among his followers, gives not of his wisdom but rather of his faith and his lovingness.

> If he is indeed wise he does not bid you enter the house of his wisdom, but rather leads you to the threshold of your own mind. (Gibran 1980, p.67)

Guiding is about enabling people through faith and love, to draw out that which lies within them. This is not to deny the sharing of information and offering of ideas and views – a position that inexperienced 'non-directive' counselors presume to be possible in their interaction with clients – rather it is to do with 'leading people to the threshold of their mind.' By 'mind' here the reference is not exclusively rationalist. Instead it speaks of the totality of our experience of being. We need to be drawn out to the very limits of our capacity if we are to experience life in its kaleidoscopic splendor and mystery. If we are to be enabled to make appropriate choices, then it will be necessary for us to experience an expansion of our awareness and a clarifying of our personhood.

The position of 'guide' differs from culture to culture. Mention has already been made of the guru to whom a devotee gives, often unflinching, obedience. A teacher in the West by no means occupies a similar position. However, it is instructive to study the art and practice of the guide in different social settings and cultural contexts.

Reconciling

Reconciling involves bringing together again parties that have become estranged or alienated from each other. These parties may range from individuals through small groups to nations. The quest, which is clearly a pastoral one, is for harmonious relations between people. It is always important to distinguish between unity and uniformity. Harmony does not imply uniformity, any more than a harmonious melody can be played using a single note. It is the very fact of diversity and difference of view that makes harmony or unity possible. The pastoral function lies in the active and creative search for means to bring people together in ways that are respectful of their differences. David Augsburger has devoted time to studying conflict resolution in different cultures. In a useful book, he explores the differences between traditional cultures and westernized ones in their conflict management strategies (Augsburger 1992). He finds that traditional cultures see conflict as a communal concern owned by groups in specific contexts. Traditional cultures prefer conflict mediation through third parties 'so that resolution is achieved in indirect, lateral, and systemic ways' (Augsburger 1992, p.8). Westernized and urbanized cultures, on the other hand, prefer direct, one-to-one engagement between the conflicted individuals: 'Individualism in life shapes individualism in strife' (p.8). Augsburger offers ways to sensitize us to pathways and patterns of conflict management through learning interculturally.

This pastoral skill is sorely needed in the world today at all levels – national, communal, inter-religious and international. Pastoral caregivers need the sensitivity to culture, faith and personality that reconciliation calls for. This lies at the heart of the purpose of God declared within the Christian message: 'God was in Christ reconciling the world to Godself' (2 Corinthians 5:19).

Nurturing

Howard Clinebell has been committed over the past several years to a form of counseling which he describes as 'Growth counseling.' This is described as

> a human-potentials approach to the helping process that defines the goal as that of facilitating the maximum development of a person's potentialities, at each life stage, in ways that contribute to the growth of others as well and to the development of a society in which all persons will have an opportunity to use their full potentialities. (Clinebell 1979, pp.17–18)

He elaborates this by pointing to six interdependent dimensions within which it is necessary for growth to occur. These are 'in our minds and in our bodies, in our relationships with other people, with the biosphere, with the groups and institutions that sustain us and in the spiritual dimension of our lives' (p.19). The function of the pastoral practitioner is to be a facilitator of growth. This is done through a process of nurture that combines caring with confrontation. Clinebell argues that growth will occur in a relationship to the extent to which caring, that is 'acceptance, affirmation, grace and love' is experienced with confrontation (openness and honesty about those aspects of reality that are being ignored or denied).

Nurturing is an ongoing process that is sensitive to the crucial 'life-stages' through which we go. These stages are times of crisis and opportunity. They require us to leave past attitudes and limitations behind and to embrace new, potentially threatening, possibilities. Here the pastoral caregiver needs skills in both comforting *and* challenging people to encourage growth.

Liberating

Internationally acclaimed Jamaican reggae artist Bob Marley, in his *Redemption Song* encourages the oppressed to emancipate themselves from mental slavery since no one apart from oneself can free one's mind. Marley thus points both to the multifaceted nature of bondage (mental slavery being one) and to the need for self-effort to shake off the shackles of slavery. There are doubtless very many levels on which it is possible for a person to experience bondage. On a 'mental' level, bondage expresses itself in an inability to think for and by one's self. People are so bound when they depend totally on others for their thinking and believing. On a 'social' level bondage can be found in the servile dependence on others in one's social circle or outside it. Dominant groups in society may suppress the views and expressions of other groups through coercion, threat and intimidation or else marginalizing or trivializing them. Domination and oppression can thus be overt or covert.

An intriguing and often perplexing aspect of domination is in the observable scenarios of 'identification with the oppressor' and 'internalization of the oppressor's views and values.' The complex reality as a result of these scenarios is that we are oftentimes confronted by persons or groups who have so internalized and identified with their oppressors that they are full of self-hatred and ambivalence about their self-worth. Such persons often aggress against others who are like themselves or their own close relations in ferocious and baffling acts of destructiveness.

Liberating involves the intricate and delicate processes of raising awareness about the sources and causes of oppression and domination in society. This entails the critical and analytic examining of both personal and structural sources, causes and developments in the establishment of current situations of inequality. In addition to awareness raising, there is the important task of considering options available for change. There is then the need for choice and action followed by reflection and evaluation.

Pastoral practitioners are called upon to be involved in social and cultural action for personal and communal liberation.

Empowering

In the process of considering options, making choices and taking relevant action, one is often confronted with the reality of questions of power. Often, marginalized groups and persons have endured years of enforced and internalized helplessness. There are, for many, real obstacles which result from what psychologist Ernest Seligman describes as 'learned helplessness.' As I have indicated, this may result from continued experiences of failing to achieve desired results in spite of pursuing the recommended paths – the oft-cited 'glass ceiling effect.' It may also be related to deficiencies in confidence, self-esteem and other personal characteristics required for effective action in the social realm.

The term 'empowerment' has been used in more recent discussions to point to the processes of revaluing self and personal characteristics together with finding and using available resources outside oneself, in such a way as to enable and motivate persons and groups to think and act in ways that will result in greater freedom and participation in the life of the societies of which they are a part. Empowering the poor has become an almost universal slogan. In the North as in the South, empowerment has been increasingly advocated in the wake of increasing poverty, polarization, marginalization and social exclusion. In the North, many Western countries are experiencing economic recession and are restructuring their economies, resulting in growing numbers of people being pushed into long-term unemployment or low-paid insecure jobs. In the South, the results of recession and restructuring are even more devastating. By the end of the 1980s, there were estimates that between 20 and 30 per cent of the world's population lived in households that were too poor to obtain the food necessary to maintain sufficient energy levels (see Craig and Mayo 1995).

Empowering takes various forms. It is seen most often as a communal affair. Some of the ways in which it expresses itself include: working together with people to attempt to restore community spirit; trying to make governments more responsive to people's needs; encouraging groups based on one or other identity issue; political education and consciousness-raising; and organizing user or service groups and en-couraging groups to develop their own alternative economic power base. Supporting and working with people in these ways can make the difference between personal well-being and psychiatric illness.

Resources

How are the functions that pastoral care exists to serve to be fulfilled? What resources are there for pastoral care? To attempt to respond to these questions, let us now examine the following resources: self-in-relationship, word, emotion, action, and symbol and imagination.

Self-in-relationship

A crucial assumption in all pastoral care is that the most important resource that care practitioners have is themselves. Training in pastoral care, if it is to be of any real effect, has to enable people to acquire the attitudes and 'ways of being with others' which will be most beneficial to the people they are with. Attitude formation involves the developing of cognitive (thinking), affective (feeling) and conative (behavior patterns) abilities. Pastoral formation necessarily is attitude formation. It is who the pastoral caregiver is, and who they are becoming, that is the crucial thing. This is especially so in the way they relate with others.

In 1988, Canadian pastoral theologian Peter Vankatwyk presented a model, which he called a Helping Style Inventory (HSI), offering a means of examining alternative ways in which carers can 'be with' their clients. He presented the HSI as a 'tool in Supervised Pastoral Education.' Essentially Vankatwyk offered a map of helping relationships based on two axes. The horizontal axis had at its opposite poles, task and person orientations. This continuum he dubbed the 'use of self' axis. On the vertical axis the question was about the 'use of power,' with a directive approach on one pole where the locus of control is external, authoritative, with deference to experts and traditions. At the other end was the facilitative use of power, appealing to internal loci of control, with reference to inner resources of wisdom and strength. By a superimposition of the two axes upon each other, Vankatwyk provided a grid showing four helping styles (Figure 4.1).

As a consequence of evaluation and testing of the original model, Vankatwyk has recently revised the designations of the styles to make them less 'potentially pejorative stereotypes' and more 'positive and creative pastoral care images,' recognizing that each of these approaches may be valid perspectives in pastoral care (Figure 4.2).

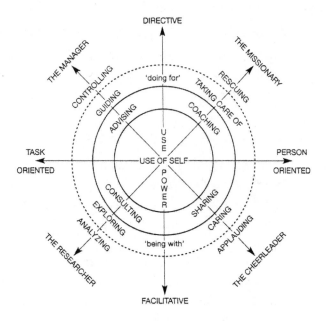

Figure 4.1 Helping style inventory map (adapted from Vankatwyk 1988, p.325)

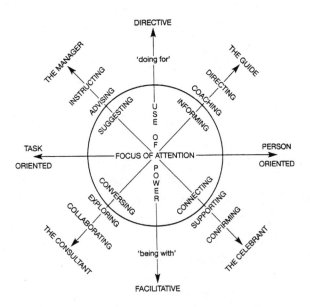

Figure 4.2 Revised helping style inventory map (adapted from Vankatwyk 1995, p.378)

The Helping styles that he offers then are:

- the *guide*, who is person-oriented and directive; he or she may inform, coach or direct as may be appropriate

- the *celebrant*, who is person-oriented and facilitative; she or he may connect with, support or confirm the person she or he is working with

- the *consultant*, who is task-oriented and facilitative; she or he converses with, explores or collaborates with a client or supervisee as needed

- the *manager*, who is task-oriented and directive; he or she may suggest to, advise or instruct the one they work with.

These titles point to 'ways of being with people' that draw on people's personality, orientation and preferred relational styles. To an extent, these are often unconscious and innate and, as such, not deliberate choices. On the other hand, where the possibility exists, persons may develop in ways that may be different from their preferences but needful if a particular situation or person is to be helped or changed.

One of the helpful aspects of Vankatwyk's revised model, within an intercultural framework, is its recognition of different styles of being pastorally related, not in a hierarchical or superior/inferior judgmental way, but rather as alternative frames relevant in different settings. Within different cultural and social locations, one or other of these styles may be the most appropriate. What is called for is the flexibility and openness to recognize, and the humility to seek to adopt, the most relevant approach.

It is a commonplace that our greatest resource in any endeavor is ourselves. However 'self' may be seen to be constituted – whether as differentially emphasized in different cultures and systems of thought, as a divine gift, a result of social construction, a work of personal effort or a composite of various personal, social and divine elements – it remains the case that what is brought into the pastoral encounter is who we are and what we are becoming; as such, that is what has to be worked with.

Word

The fascination with narrative as category for and of investigation continues to be evident in a wide range of disciplines from literary theory through history, theology and anthropology. Many pastoral writers have observed on the great relevance and significance of words in pastoral care. Deeks (1987) begins his book on pastoral theology with an examination of how storytelling and conversation can be of value in pastoral care. Pattison (1989) makes an analysis of 'conversation' as a useful way of conceptualizing and engaging in theological reflection upon pastoral practice. Ed Wimberly (1991) is convinced and convincing on the manner in which Black pastors approach pastoral care through narrative. Berinyuu (1989) argues that storytelling is part of the 'psychodrama of everyday life in Africa.' In each of these analyses, arising from culturally very diverse situations, supreme value is placed on a person's ability and freedom to verbalize their life experience. The expression in words of thoughts, feelings and action may have cathartic value, especially where their expression has been, for any number of reasons inhibited, suppressed, misunderstood or misinterpreted. The pastoral care practitioner then becomes a 'story-listener, story-stimulator, story-interpreter and story prohibitor.' (as explored by Jones 1991).

In the story-listening role, the pastoral caregiver enables people to hear their own story aloud, to hear it for themselves and thus possibly obtain a more objective view of who they are in their multifaceted complexity. Listening is a core skill in any form of caring. Gerkin (1984) has argued that selfhood is closely linked up with having a story line. He writes, 'to tell a story is to have a self and to lose the sense of story line of one's life is to lose the sense of being a self' (p.211). As a story-stimulator a pastoral caregiver may, by encouraging and asking questions, help a person begin again to weave a thread through their life.

Every story is, naturally, an interpretation. The telling of a story entails, among others, the selection, ordering and emphasizing of events in such a way as to make a coherent and meaningful sequence that may be tragic, comic or indifferent, or combinations of these. A pastoral caregiver is as such involved as she participates as listener or stimulator, in a process of interpretation and reinterpretation. This role has, of course, been, and is being, played by therapists and counselors. Different pastoral practitioners have understood the 'interpretation' task in relation to the grand stories of the community of faith that the caregivers belong to. For Bohler (1987), it has to do with the provision of an alternative framework, a 'twist in the meaning' of the story. For Foskett and Lyall (1988), in a book that explores the model of 'story' within a pastoral supervisory context, the pastoral carer is a bearer of the 'gospel story', which interacts with and is interacted with by the stories of all the participants. Bohler argues that a pastoral carer may, however, also act as a story inhibitor, where storytelling replaces or serves to avoid present action. Her concern is where people with addictions, for example, use stories as diversionary tactics to avoid doing something about their condition. Jacobs (1988a, 1988b), on the other hand, is convinced that no story is irrelevant and no material is to be prohibited. For, in clearly psychodynamic as well as Christian theological terms, 'freely chosen stories nevertheless contain clues to the present, if only we had ears to hear' (p.17).

Clearly much of pastoral care will entail conversation, speech and listening. Reading and reflection on prose, poetry or fiction also provides an opportunity for care to be mediated. The resource of words will doubtless continue to be an important one in pastoral care. Questions need to be raised, though, about the place of language in pastoral care. One of the features of the globalization identified earlier as a trend in the movement for pastoral care and counseling, is the dominance of the English language. While language can be a great unifier, a kind of social glue within community, and can enhance communication across cultural boundaries, it is also true that it can be the cause of misunderstanding, deep hurt, oppression, marginalization and exclusion. To be able to express oneself in a language in which one is fluent can be most therapeutic. However, this can be an alienating experience if no one understands what one says. To find another person who speaks and understands ones own language can be the greatest of relief. On the other hand, as all travellers in foreign lands find, the inability to find understanding of one's needs can be akin to inhabiting the strange inner world of the schizophrenic.

Each specific language has particular strengths and weaknesses in conveying particular ideas, concepts, thoughts and feelings. This is evident most sharply in translations from language to language. But is also present even where languages appear to be similar, for example British English and American English.

Pastoral care seeks to mediate and communicate love across barriers and between people. As such, attention needs to be paid to the importance of language in pastoral care. Questions about the form of language, including the issues of dialect, intonation, choice of expression, familiarity with particular idioms, as well as meaning, need to be faced. Intercultural pastoral carer practitioners will need critically to examine their practice with regards to language.

Emotion

The ability to feel is one of the aspects of life that, while being recognized and exploited in several forms of everyday life, has been either ignored or else suppressed in many religious circles. Feeling is the characteristic of living from which we are told we have the most to fear. Emotionalism, deception, seduction, irrationality and loss of control are often presented as the results of attending to feeling. At the same time, advertisers exploit our desires, our sexuality and our love of pleasure for the marketing and sale of everything from toothpaste to cars.

Without emotion, *empathy, warmth* and *genuineness* – the therapeutic triad spoken of in counseling and psychotherapy – would be impossible. Feeling permits us to be sensitive, caring and to 'understand the experiences' of others. It is by feeling that we enter into the 'world' of others, whether through their writing or their speech. Great music appeals to our ability to be aroused and moved through a combination of deep, wild and calm, peaceful passions. The esthetic quality of life by which we are able to determine what to us is beautiful or desirable depends not so much on thought or language as on feeling. Art and poetry are evocative of feeling and similarly appeal to our emotional makeup through the unusual, unexpected or strange usage of media. It is an artist's or poet's ability to surprise through depiction or portrayal of his or her own thoughts, feelings or observations that makes the difference between good, bad and indifferent work. The artist's portrayal of the familiar in evocative or else soothing ways appeals to our feelings about life and our surroundings. Motivation to thought or action can be seen to lie in that which moves or inspires our feelings.

As such, it is to be expected that feeling is an important resource for pastoral care and counseling. Pastoral practitioners need to develop their abilities of sensitivity and empathy through attention to their own feelings. It is as pastoral caregivers get in closer touch with their own feelings of hurt and pain, sorrow and sadness that they can begin to approach the pain of others. Moreover, feelings of pleasure and joy, arousal and elation may also put carers in touch with those they care for in the rich variety of the emotional tapestry of life.

Action

Deeks (1987) makes a distinction between 'action' and 'activity.' An action is the concrete, measurable event by which we seek to achieve a particular goal. An activity, on the other hand, is something we engage in as an end in itself. For Deeks, activities, such as running to keep fit or listening to music, may serve 'subjective purposes,' and at this point the distinction becomes blurred. Whilst the distinction may be difficult to sustain, the analysis is helpful, particularly because it introduces the important factors of motivation and purpose necessary in any analysis of action.

Pastoral action is, in my view, purposeful activity. When pastors listen, they do so because listening to another is a valuable and important activity in itself. At the same time, listening enables both speaker and listener to get in touch with what may well be the core of a person's need. When a pastor is present with another in the silence of care, the silence may in truth be the most powerful life-giving activity possible.

Pastoral action may also take the form of a concrete, measurable event. When pastors offer food to the hungry, clothe the naked or provide shelter for the roofless, they engage in action that is both meaningful and necessary. It is important that pastoral care be seen as entailing both concrete, measurable action as well as intangible, reflective activity.

Symbol and imagination

There are, of course, very many different ways in which the word *symbol* is itself used. Ernest Jones, who made many of the works of Freud available in English, offered some classic psychoanalytic thoughts on symbolism. Writing in 1916, Jones distinguished between a wide, general meaning including anything of a figurative nature, and a psychoanalytic meaning in which symbolism always involved regression to a more simple way of apprehending reality. In the latter view, symbols always represent ideas about the self, an immediate blood relative or something to do with birth, love or death. Most important in this view, is that symbols always involve the psychological process of repression of thoughts, feelings and behaviors associated with the symbolized ideas.

Jung had a very different view on the function of symbols. For him, the ability to symbolize provides a bridge between the conscious and the unconscious mind, thus furthering the development of the psyche. As such, far from being repressive and regressive, symbols for Jung are creative and facilitative of worthwhile living.

Paul Ricoeur, offers an intermediate position between Freud and Jung. Ricoeur,

> acknowledges the archaic instinctual underlay of the symbol, in agreement with the Freudian position, but maintains that each symbol takes up a preceding one 'to deny and overcome it,' so that there is a progressive self-transformation of symbols in a telic direction. (Martyn 1992, pp.58–59)

Language is perhaps a primary form of symbolism, but so is the art, that seems to have been a part of humanity from prehistoric times. Some would argue that such art is a pre-lingual form of communication. Literature can also be understood as a major form of symbolism. Ernst Cassirer in his *Philosophy of Symbolic Forms* (1955) demonstrated that symbolic forms such as language provide the means of apprehending reality. Melanie Klein, whose work advanced the Object Relations School of psychoanalysis, points out that the ability to symbolize is the basis of all creativity and of those skills by which we relate to the world around us.

Existentialist psychotherapist Rollo May (1961) provides valuable empirical evidence, with reference to the work of Kurt Goldstein with wartime brain-injured patients, that shows that the capacity to symbolize is definitional of human persons *as* persons. May expresses most clearly what appears to be the gathered wisdom of many writers from different disciplines who have explored the significance of symbols:

> The symbol is a 'bridging act', a bridging of the gap between outer existence (the world) and inner meaning, and it arose out of man's [sic] capacity to separate inner meaning and outer existence. (May 1961, p.21)

Child therapist, Dorothy Martyn has also more recently investigated this capacity in its developmental framework and as a result is able to point out that 'not only do the beginnings of symbolic thought and the beginnings of human relatedness coincide, but that the development of both also coincide' (Martyn 1992, p.67).

The work of British psychoanalyst and pediatrician, D.W. Winnicott points clearly in the direction of the importance of symbolization in human relatedness. A child's ability to move from the object as *equivalent* to what it stands for into play in which an object *represents* what it stands for, is crucial for healthy development. It was theologian Paul Tillich who argued further that symbols not only 'point to' but also in various ways 'participate in' what they symbolize.

Thus the characteristically human ability to symbolize enables us to relate to the external world of persons and objects, sharing in communities of meaning and significance, and imaginatively represent and participate in what we symbolize. This capacity in many cultures is put to use in matters of social and communal interest. As I have shown elsewhere, linguists (spokespeople for traditional rulers) in traditional Ghanaian society, have staves or umbrella tops sculpted or designed in the form of human beings, animals, plants or parts of objects, in order to symbolize and convey the political values of traditional society. Three examples should suffice to emphasize the importance of the sense of community in Ghanaian traditional society (see Lartey 1987).

1. A hand holding an egg, usually found atop a linguist's staff means 'Power is like holding an egg, if you hold it too tightly it breaks and if you hold it too loosely it drops.' This sculpture is often prominently displayed when politicians and others are invested with governing authority. The significance of this sculpture is that authority, especially political authority, must be handled with care.

2. A double head with each face pointing in the opposite direction says: One head does not constitute a council. The importance of this is that it reminds people that wisdom requires looking in many directions and eliciting the views of more than one person.

3. A man trying to scrape herbal medicine from the bark of a tree by himself finds that the shavings fall out of his receptacle. This emphasizes the need for cooperation, for the man would find

the work easier if there was another person with him, to hold the receptacle for him.

The capacity to creatively and imaginatively enter into and draw on the symbolizing ability which human persons, as individuals and social groups, possess is a vital resource in pastoral care.

This brings us to the end of our consideration of the functions of and resources for intercultural pastoral care. In the next chapter we shall be taking a close look at counseling, a major form which pastoral care has taken, especially in the Western world and those countries that have been significantly influenced by the West.

PART II

Private Care and Public Struggle

CHAPTER 5

Counseling as Pastoral Care and Pastoral Counseling

Counseling

Counseling and psychotherapy occupy a central place in Western approaches to pastoral care. Under the influence of discernible social, political, ideological and cultural trends, post-Enlightenment Western society seemed to have developed an approach to dealing with the personal, emotional and relational ills that beset individuals. Psychology, which by the early part of the twentieth century was enjoying a distinct and arguably scientific status, and particularly the subdiscipline of psychotherapy, offered a feasible, socially and scientifically acceptable alternative to religion in dealing with the perplexities of life. As Halmos (1965) has argued, the values and ideals espoused by the counseling profession seemed well suited for a post-Christian, post-political society (see also Clebsch and Jaekle 1967). They provided a way of being loving, helpful and kind without being religious.

It is instructive to note some of the core values which make counseling appear to 'fit Western industrialized society' (Wilson 1988, following Lambourne). First, a focus on the individual means that it is the dignity, worth and uniqueness of each individual as an individual which lies at the heart of counseling theory and practice. Second, there is a valuing of verbal expressiveness. Counseling is based on the skilled and careful use of relationship, within which conditions are created to facilitate the expression of thoughts and feelings and the exploration of behavioural patterns which may be causing concern. It is the ability freely to express and explore thoughts, feelings and behavior that makes the counseling process 'work.' Third, and related to this is, a focus on client self-disclosure.

There is an implied imbalance of power in counseling since the client (the needy one) seeks out the counselor (the one who helps) even where serious efforts are made, as within 'person-centered' approaches, to recognize that the client is in a very real sense 'the expert.' So that even though the counselor may at times and for specific limited reasons self-disclose, it is the client's self-disclosure that constitutes the raw material upon which the counseling process is based. Fourth, the gaining of knowledge or insight is an expressed aim of most forms of counseling. The theoretical and interpretive frames underlying counseling approaches may differ markedly from one to another. The overt aims of strict behaviorist approaches are behavioral change rather than mere insight. However, they all make use of communication and relational skills, which would be fairly meaningless without the transmission and gaining of some form of knowledge. Fifth, is the use of cause–effect interpretive theories. By and large, counselors tend to explore and explain phenomena within specific frameworks in keeping with preferred theories of human nature, growth and development.

What then is counseling? How do counselors explain their activities?

Counselling is the skilled and principled use of relationship to facilitate self-knowledge, emotional acceptance and growth, and the optimal development of personal resources. The overall aim is to provide an opportunity to work towards living more satisfyingly and resourcefully.

At least so says the British Association for Counselling (BAC). The BAC goes on to say:

People become engaged in counselling when a person, occupying regularly or temporarily the role of counsellor offers or agrees explicitly to offer time, attention and respect to another person or persons temporarily in the role of client. The task of counselling is to give the client an opportunity to explore, discover and clarify ways of living more resourcefully and towards greater well-being. (BAC 1991)

Counselors then, adopt particular ways of relating and responding to persons (clients), which entail the giving of time, attention and respect to these persons. Counselors use relationship in a skilled, principled and purposeful fashion. The aims of their endeavors are that clients be enabled to explore their thoughts, feelings and behavior; to reach clearer knowledge and understanding of themselves; and as a result find the strength and resources to cope more effectively with life.

Counseling relationships will vary according to need but may be concerned with developmental issues, addressing and resolving specific problems, making decisions, coping with crisis, developing personal insights and knowledge, working through feelings of inner conflict or improving relationships with others (BAC 1991).

Models of counseling

It is possible to categorize counseling approaches for purposes of discussion, into four broad streams. In the nature of things, some approaches could be classified, depending on which aspects of it are emphasized, into more than one of the following categories. Moreover, the streams are not mutually exclusive and there certainly are degrees of overlap. The categories are:

- insight-oriented
- behavioristic
- relationship-oriented
- transpersonal.

Let us now discuss each of these in turn.

INSIGHT-ORIENTED APPROACHES

These essentially aim at helping people gain insight into the nature and development of their problems. Each has a particular theory of human growth and development and, by implication, views about causes and courses of difficulties in the development process. These theories provide an interpretive frame along which trained counselors explore and seek to facilitate the gaining of insight within their clients. The overarching view is that when persons know more constructively what the, often hidden, inner dynamics of their lives are, they can be enabled to structure the processes of living in a more satisfactory or creative fashion.

The main theorists here would draw their inspiration from the psychoanalytic tradition pioneered by Sigmund Freud and variously developed and deviated from, by post-Freudians such as Carl Jung, Alfred Adler and Otto Rank. The Object Relations School of Melanie Klein,

Karen Horney, and others, has developed in ways that have reassessed some of the core concepts of the psychoanalytic movement while remaining broadly in sympathy with the approach of seeking insight.

BEHAVIORISTIC OR LEARNING-THEORY-ORIENTED APPROACHES

The basic premise upon which learning theory is based is that all behavior is learned, and that all learning is the result of reinforced practice. As a consequence of this, learning-theory-based approaches to counseling aim at helping people to change their behavior through the application of principles of learning. Essentially what is being claimed here is that if persons can be motivated to act in different ways, their confusion or dissatisfaction will tend to dissipate and the problem will have been dealt with. Explanations are not sought in speculative theories of origin, development or causation. Rather attention is paid to the unwanted behavioral patterns and the schedules of reinforcement that keep them in place. Strategies are then adopted which will directly affect these behaviors, to weaken the established stimulus–response chains and to replace them with more desired behaviors.

Strict behaviorists such as American psychologist B.F. Skinner, William Glasser (who founded reality therapy) and Joseph Wolpe (who originated the highly successful method of systematic desensitization for the treatment of phobias) focus almost exclusively on overt observable behaviors. Cognitive behaviorists, on the other hand, broaden the definition of behavior to include 'covert behaviors' like thinking and believing. Rational-emotive therapy, originated by Albert Ellis, and Aaron Beck's cognitive therapy would be examples of cognitive-behavioristic approaches.

RELATIONSHIP-ORIENTED APPROACHES

The underlying assumption of all relationship-oriented approaches is that human persons are relational beings. In order to understand persons, therefore, it is necessary to explore the relational patterns by which they were socialized, to gauge the extent to which these have been internalized in direct or modified forms, and to examine the nature of the network of current relationships within which an individual is embedded. It is envisaged that in the counseling encounter a client may be set free from debilitating patterns of behavior by experiencing understanding and acceptance and is thus enabled to renew broken relationships with self and others.

Relationship-oriented approaches may further be subdivided into

1. human potentials approaches

2. radical and systemic approaches.

Human potentials approaches express an explicit goal of 'actualizing' a person's full potential. American humanistic psychologist Abraham Maslow (1908–1970) can be credited with the advancing of the idea of *self-actualization*. Like Carl Rogers, supreme illustrator of this approach and originator of client-centered psychotherapy, Maslow, in his early works, was imbued with highly optimistic and humane views of human nature undergirded with a spirit of scientific enquiry. Maslow's pyramidal hierarchy of human needs, beginning with basic safety and security needs and rising once these have been fulfilled to esthetic needs, is now very familiar to many. His later interest in 'transpersonal' psychology was still very much with a view to exploring human potentials such as creativeness, beauty, value, imagination and joy.

Carl Rogers was convinced that no matter how deprived the early experience of a human person, she had within her a potential and a drive to fulfill her potential. The role of the counselor was to create the requisite environment, through relating with the client in open, accepting and warm ways, within which such potential would be realized. Brian Thorne, a leading figure in person-centered counseling in Britain, articulates the following philosophy: 'God is trustworthy, the body is trustworthy, desires are trustworthy, sexuality is not a problem, survival is not a problem, death is not to be dreaded' (Thorne 1991, p.80).

Eric Berne's transactional analysis is a particularly intriguing 'human potentials' approach. Based on views of the structure of human personality that bear resemblance to Freudian constructs, Berne's work examines the patterns of interaction and relationship characteristic of a person and proposes a very optimistic, though not unrealistic, way of working with people which has proved adaptable to a huge range of human relations settings. Transactional analysis is in my view, a predominantly relation-oriented human-potentials approach that has very wide applicability.

Fritz Perls' Gestalt therapy adopts a radically different style of client–counselor relationship from that of Rogers or Berne. In Gestalt therapy, the counselor deliberately frustrates all attempts on the part of the client to be dependent on the counselor. Instead the counselor encourages complete responsibility and choice of response in the client. In this way, it is believed that the client will develop independence and self-directedness – very desirable goals within a Western industrialized context. Gestalt therapy then, in a rather particular manner, places optimum faith in human capability and personal responsibility, and seeks to promote these through confrontational forms of relationship.

Radical and systemic approaches focus on changing social systems so that all their members will be freer to grow towards wholeness. The objective in view is to facilitate creative change in relationships and in social systems. Various forms of family therapy would be examples of this approach. The characteristic orientation of family therapists, and indeed the main locus of their therapeutic attention, is towards the interpersonal processes and behaviors occurring, not within but rather between the members of a family.

The common motif in all radical therapies is the conviction that personal growth and social change are inextricably linked. Feminist therapies are in the forefront of a necessary shift in therapeutic focus and practice. Women live in societies that exert very significant influences upon them. It is crucial to understand the interactions between the inner and outer worlds when women present for counseling. Often the source of the issues at stake, though its manifestation might be within the inner, emotional life of the client, lies in the outer social world of expectations, socialization and roles. As such, the political, social and historical structures, as well as individual dynamics, need to be addressed (see e.g. Walker 1992).

TRANSPERSONAL OR SPIRITUAL-GROWTH-ORIENTED APPROACHES

Transpersonal psychology grew out of humanistic psychology with the express purpose of studying what are evidently human experiences that had been ruled out of court by experimental psychology. It was Maslow who insisted that the 'self' had needs for stimulation, enhancement of experience and for stimulation. Indeed he was sure that desires for self-transcendence were not only real but also merited serious attention. Transpersonal psychologists study altered states of consciousness, the effects of psychotropic drugs, meditation and various Eastern religious practices.

As a parallel development, transpersonal psychotherapists regard spiritual growth as central and essential in all therapy or counseling. All such therapists have their own particular understanding of what 'spiritual' growth might be. But they are united in the view that spiritual growth is crucial to the therapeutic process.

Three examples of therapies which might be classified as transpersonal are:

1. The work of Holocaust survivor Viktor Frankl – which he dubbed *logotherapy*.

2. Carl Gustav Jung's individuation.

3. Italian psychiatrist Roberto Assagioli's *psychosynthesis*.

Indeed Assagioli summed up the case pictorially and succinctly when he said, in an interview not long before his death:

> In one of his letters Freud said, 'I'm interested only in the basement of the human building.' We try to build an elevator which will allow a person access to every level of his personality. After all, a building with only a basement is very limited. We want to open up the terrace where you can sun-bathe or look at the stars. Our concern is the synthesis of all areas of the personality. This means psychosynthesis is holistic, global and inclusive. It is not against psychoanalysis or even behaviour modification, but it insists that the need for meaning, for higher values, for a spiritual life, are as real as biological or social needs. (quoted in Clinebell 1981, p.265)

Viktor Frankl's therapeutic work was premised upon the sense that it is impossible to understand human beings as human unless one takes into account the human need for *meaning* and *purpose*. Jung argues that individuation, the coming to selfhood, can be likened to a religious experience. It is an integration of the disparate dimensions of a person's conscious and unconscious life into a whole that enables one to function meaningfully.

It is necessary to realize that many forms of counseling within a religious framework may be seen as forms of transpersonal counseling. Spiritual direction, widely practiced within the Roman Catholic tradition, could be classified as an example of this approach to counseling. But also *guidance* within Islam and the *mentoring* of the Hindu guru employ a similar orientation. This is because the goal and center of such activities is spiritual growth, described in particular ways consonant with the beliefs of the particular religious tradition.

To understand the place and function of the guru it is necessary not merely to savor popular Western stereotypes but rather to recognize the profoundly Indian origin, development and practice of this form of transpersonal counseling. The guru is often called in India a *jnani* or 'realized soul' – one who knows and has experienced the presence of God within. In the strands of Hinduism where a vision of God is the *moksha* (state of absolute release) that is sought, the most celebrated guru is undoubtedly Krishna, who in the *Bhagavad Gita* appears as the charioteer of the young soldier Arjuna. Krishna is really an incarnation of the great god Vishnu. The unfolding relationship between Krishna and his pupil Arjuna, which climaxes in a theophany in which Krishna reveals himself in all his glory to a devoted Arjuna, is an illuminating depiction of the teacher–disciple encounter in the Hindu conception.

Transpersonal counseling is a form of pastoral care. In my view, it may be distinguished from pastoral counseling, even if in practice it is often inseparable. Before we discuss pastoral counseling in greater detail, let us examine the characteristics of counseling.

Characteristics of counseling

In order to further clarify our discussion of the practice of counseling it is necessary to examine some core characteristics of the process. These characteristics are the skills which trainees are schooled into and constitute the ingredients, to borrow a culinary metaphor, which are considered essential to the effective practice of most forms of counseling. These characteristics tend to be expressed in nonverbal ways, such as through gestures, posture, tone of voice and facial expression. They are thus closely related to the skills of effective interpersonal communication. I will explore ten characteristics:

1. listening

2. empathy

3. interpathy

4. respect

5. non-possessive warmth

6. genuineness

7. concreteness

8. confrontation

9. confidentiality

10. immediacy.

LISTENING

At the very heart of all forms of counseling lies the ability to listen. Listening has been described as being silent with another person in an active way, silently receiving what another human person has to say. Listening, unlike other forms of silence though, requires that the listener be open and active, not asleep or dead. The true listener is quiet and yet sensitive, open, receptive and alive to the one listened to.[1]

One of the major obstacles to listening is talking. This takes the form of the inability actually to stop speaking or else the 'inner talking' that continually interrupts the flow of the speech of the other, especially where one disagrees, by inner responses of disagreement or counterargument. German theologian Dietrich Bonhoeffer, who was killed for his opposition to Hitler, was very concerned that often Christian ministers suffered from this malady. He wrote:

> It is his work we do for our brother when we learn to listen to him. Christians, especially ministers, so often think they must always contribute something when they are in the company of others, that this is the one service they have to render. They forget that listening can be a greater service than speaking. Many people are looking for an ear that will listen. They do not find it among Christians, because these Christians are talking where they should be listening... In the end there is nothing left

but spiritual chatter and clerical condescension arrayed in pious words. (Bonhoeffer 1954, pp.87–88)[2]

Too much chatter, as an observable social fact, may achieve the same result as isolation. It may obstruct real contact with other persons by preventing them from making real contact with us.

Listening requires deep inner security and strength. People who cannot read authors or listen to speakers with whom they disagree, often display a lack of inner poise. They must fight with the author whose ideas they do not share or the person who has done things they disapprove of. Often this is a display of fear that the ground may be swept from under their feet or that their own views might be found wanting or else that they might be changed.

A first step in listening, then, is allowing oneself to be with another person and to be completely silent with them. Silent not only with one's lips but also in one's inner response – neither agreeing nor disagreeing with what they have to say. Listening openly and permitting the other person to be what they are, freely, without controlling, coercing or censoring what they say. This clearly is a skill which has to be developed and is very much more complex than the 'just listening' of everyday conversation.

The person who listens actively and creatively, however, does not remain silent throughout the process. There comes a time when the listener reflects with the other person, seeking to clarify what has been heard. This may be done by a process of paraphrasing or summarizing and checking to see whether what has been received corresponds with what was intended. The creative listener may amplify or sharpen what has been heard and ask the speaker to verify whether that is what it feels like to them. An active listener may ask for more detail or for a retelling of aspects of what has been said so that what is in the speaker is allowed to be expressed in all its fullness and complexity. Such enquiring is done with 'open' questions. A closed question can be responded to with a 'yes' or a 'no' and is often a leading question (e.g. 'Were you at the party that night?'). An open question, on the other hand, opens up the discussion by enabling the speaker to choose what is of interest and significance for them (e.g. 'How was the party that night?'). It is important that it be borne in mind that such questioning is not voyeuristic nor is it to satisfy the curiosity of the listener.

It aims at the ventilation of feelings, to be borne with care, concern and sensitivity by both persons in the counseling relationship.

When listening is deep, real and penetrating, the experience can be awe-inspiring, for it has to do with core being-in-encounter. Listeners enter into a holy sacred space where personal, intimate material is brought into play. But this level of encounter is seldom reached until listeners have been willing to hear about all the petty concerns and interests of the other. Listeners must listen to mundane descriptions of events and experiences which seemingly have no earth-shattering significance, but which have been meaningful for the speaker. Such meaning could be ingrained within feelings of sadness, sorrow or joy and elation. More often than not, though, meaning emerges from the most ordinary encounters of life.

Most people who encounter listeners do not immediately bare their souls to them. The tendency seems to be to test out the waters to see just how deep they run. If openness, sensitivity and care are encountered, this seems to encourage people slowly and gradually to begin to go on to the more significant or baffling matters. The guilt, fear, anxieties, faults, pain and loneliness are reserved for those listeners who seem secure enough within themselves, and open enough to be alongside persons for more than a superficial scratching.

Many of the essential features of active listening have been captured in the following acronym:

Look and be interested

Inquire with open questions

Stay alive to the speaker

Test your understanding by checking

Empathize

Neutralize your feelings

EMPATHY

A man should not advise another man till he has walked a mile in his moccasins.

(Native American saying)

It is believed that the term *empathy* was first used in the 1930s by C.R. Shaw in describing his work with 'problem' boys in Chicago. Empathy, according to Shaw, enables the worker to see life 'as the boy conceives it, rather than as an adult might imagine it, by entering into the boy's experience.'

Carl Rogers presented the following classic, technical definition of empathy:

> The ability to perceive the internal frame of reference of another with accuracy and with the emotional components and meanings which pertain thereto, as if one were the other person, but without ever losing the 'as if' condition. (Rogers 1975, p.140)

Empathy entails entering into another person's thought patterns, inner feelings and ways of understanding the world. Egan (1986) describes it as 'the ability to enter into and understand the world of another person and to communicate this understanding to him or her' (p.95). Empathy has been understood as having the three characteristics of all attitudes, namely, a *feeling* (affective) level, a *thinking* (cognitive) level and a *tendency to action* (conative) level. Empathy then, is a way of being with other people, which enters into how it feels like to be who they are. Empathy as a cognitive process involves professional contact with persons that appreciates and understands the nuances and complexities of their lives from their point of view. On the action-orientation level, empathy is a communication process in which thoughts, understandings and shared feelings are exchanged.

Empathy involves an accurate awareness of another person's feelings, the ability to 'stay with' these feelings no matter how painful or inexplicable, and being able to express or enable their expression. For this to happen, the person empathizing has to retain their own identity and inner strength. Rogers' 'as if' quality must remain the mark of empathy in order that the counselor is not swamped or engulfed by the torrents of the client's feelings. Empathy is not the same as identification. The counselor does not 'become' the client. Lee (1968) puts it this way: 'To understand the other from within rather than from without, yet to carry into the identification (the counsellor's) own strength and maturity' (p.46). The word *identification* in this rendering may be misleading for the one who empathizes remains a distinct person. It is necessary to maintain the distance which preserves the integrity and distinct personhood of both counselor and client. The counselor, as a separate person, attempts to 'enter into' the experience of another person (the client) and to understand what it feels like to be 'them.'

Empathy seldom happens instantaneously. It may involve a slow and painful process of traveling intensely and carefully with the other person. There may be periods of confusion, uncertainty and misunderstanding. In some situations, empathy may be impossible to achieve. However, even such recognition may be valuable if acknowledged.

Empathy has been distinguished from sympathy. Sympathy, in this sense, has connotations of pity and condescension. The 'strong' sympathize with the 'weak.' Such feelings may be emotionally satisfying for the sympathizer but they often undermine the confidence and weaken the ability of the object of sympathy. If sympathy is a feeling *for* someone in their predicament, empathy, on the other hand, is a feeling *with* the other that recognizes both weakness and strength within that other person.

INTERPATHY

Augsburger introduced the term *interpathy* to attempt to reflect what needs to happen when empathy crosses cultural boundaries. This is the way he explains it.

> *Interpathy* is an intentional cognitive envisioning and affective experiencing of another's thoughts and feelings, even though the thoughts rise from another process of knowing, the values grow from another frame of moral reasoning and the feelings spring from another basis of assumptions. (Augsburger 1986, p.29)

Interpathy involves 'bracketing' one's own beliefs and values and temporarily entering a very different world of beliefs and values. Such ability is required of the historian, anthropologist and translator. By the same token, anyone who reads a novel set in a different time period or country has, to some extent, to exercise 'interpathy.'

Augsburger argues that in interpathic caring, a culturally different person seeks to 'fully entertain' within their awareness 'a foreign belief.' He continues:

I (the culturally different person) take a foreign perspective, base my thought on a foreign assumption, and allow myself to feel the resultant feelings and their cognitive and emotive consequences in my personality as I inhabit, insofar as I am capable of inhabiting, a foreign context (Augsburger 1986, p.30)

This is a radical and serious attempt to engage across cultural boundaries. It seeks not only to recognize and respect another in their 'otherness' but also to attempt to *share* that otherness in as much as one is able to. It is a crucial extension of the valuable characteristic of empathy into the realms of intercultural work.

For interpathy to function, though, it is necessary to recognize that it rests upon the premise of human universality, which we have argued is an essential aspect of an intercultural vision. We can attempt to cross cultural boundaries precisely because those who inhabit the other side are equally human. This is the basic stance, which consequently requires us to take the otherness of the other seriously. It is because 'they' are human that we seek to share in their thoughts, feelings and behavior – no matter how different. Moreover, when 'we' cross over we must be careful not to think that the people we encounter will all in every way fit in with the ideas we have about 'those people.' What we should expect, because this is the case with all human societies, is to find living human persons in all their rich and colorful diversity, influenced no doubt as we are, by dominant as well as subdominant cultural forces and not some colorless, stereotypical clones all singing the same tune, thinking the same thoughts and behaving in identical ways.

RESPECT

In counseling the belief that 'the client knows best' is not simply an advertising ploy aimed at attracting unsuspecting customers into purchasing things they do not need and will probably never use. In person-centered psychotherapy and counseling, it is the cornerstone upon which theory and practice is based. Rogers' technical expression for this characteristic was 'unconditional positive regard.' Counselors *respect* their clients in the sense that they value them as persons of worth and dignity. There is a deliberate choice on the part of the counselor to presuppose a measure of integrity and love of truth in every client. Respect implies a deep valuing of the full personhood and otherness of the client, no matter how distorted it may appear to be. Counselors esteem clients as worthy of complete and serious attention in their individual uniqueness. The client is seen as having the resources of self-determination and inner-directedness necessary to manage their lives more effectively. As such the counselor seeks to create a relationship of rapport and trust within which clients feel free to be exactly who they are without fear of blame for their feelings or thoughts. In this way, it can be said that the counselor seeks to be *for* the client.

This stance may appear at times to be the worst form of wishful thinking in a world in which personal and moral fallibility is paraded in the newspapers daily, demonstrating how cruel, callous and destructive human persons can be. It is perhaps true that the origins of this stance in counseling owes a lot to the optimistic heady days of the initiation of humanistic psychology and client-centered counseling in the US in the 1950s and 1960s. Advocates of the importance of respect in counseling have argued that 'being for the client' is both gracious *and* toughminded. It is gracious in the sense that it responds to clients in their basic humanity which is deemed to be valuable and good. It is toughminded in its expectation that clients will be prepared to work toward the realization of their potential where blocks and undesirable qualities are discernible. Respect, then, is not some kind of sentimental, mushy or 'gooey' wide-eyed, narcissistic admiration of the client. Instead it seeks in a down-to-earth manner to orient both client and counselor to that which is of worth and value within all humanity in order to enable the necessary confrontation of that which is not.

In this regard, aspects of philosophical theology might perhaps be valuable. In a sense the respect which counselors seek is premised on the idea that *esse qua esse bonum est* (being as being is good). In Christian thought this is an affirmation of the Jewish story of the creation of the world by God in which God declares all God has created to be 'very good.' As such there is an *essential* goodness that lies at the heart of all creation. However, the presence of evil in humanity is an *existential* reality that must be faced squarely, regardless of how one conceptualizes its origins.[3] By choosing to demonstrate 'respect' for all clients, counselors choose to come to the existential through the essential, to proceed from the 'image of God' to the 'fallenness of humanity.'

Respect is fundamental to intercultural counseling. As a matter of fact, its absence nullifies any form of intercultural work. In a world where, as psychological research has shown, much interpersonal perception is based on nonverbal cues,[4] and which has historically and currently become highly 'racialized,' it is crucial that counselors and clients examine their attitudes to each other where they differ from each other along the skin-color dimension.[5] Carter (1995) has argued that 'race is perhaps the most visible of all cultural differences (in America)... and has been and continues to be the ultimate measure of social exclusion and inclusion, because it is a visible factor that historically and currently determines the rules and bounds of social and cultural interaction' (p.3). He therefore argues on the basis of carefully examined empirical evidence that instead of denying or ignoring race, an approach which promotes only confusion and conflict, counselors and psychotherapists need to 'discuss, understand and integrate' race as an accepted part of our psychosocial development. Carter's work shows the need for truthful respect in working with all people.[6]

NON-POSSESSIVE WARMTH

A characteristic of counseling that lies more in the spheres of personality and feeling is 'warmth.' Essentially, warmth in counseling is a welcoming and loving attitude toward a client in which the client is affirmed and accepted as a person. The Rogerian term for this would be 'unconditional acceptance.' Warmth is a deep and genuine care for the person as person that is not based on an evaluation of the client's feelings, thoughts or behavior. Instead it is the 'fellow-feeling' that is generated by encounter with another full-blooded human person.

There are two qualifiers that are a necessary part of warmth. The first is that it is 'non-possessive.' Warmth can be contaminated by feelings and desires of affection that wish to 'hold on' to the client and in some sense retain them within one's emotional hold. Complications of a sexual nature may be involved in this kind of possessiveness. Second, and on the other hand, there may be feelings of dislike or even revulsion. In such cases, it is tempting within particular cultural settings to attempt to display 'standard counselor warmth' or 'role' warmth. These stilted activities are most inappropriate for the kind of relationship that counseling is, since such put-up jobs undercut genuine interaction.

In psychodynamic approaches to counseling, feelings of attraction or revulsion would be considered within the nexus of transference and countertransference. Transference, according to Michael Jacobs, a leading trainer in psychodynamic counseling in Britain, refers to 'the repetition by the client of old child-like patterns of relating to significant people, such as parents, but now seen in relation to the counsellor' (Jacobs 1992, p.12). Countertransference is the reverse side of transference 'that is, feelings evoked *in the counsellor* by the client'(Jacobs 1992, p.106; see also Symington 1986, pp.106–112). Initially seen as problematic, exploring the transference became for Freud and his followers the crucial key to the therapeutic relationship. Transference and countertransference form a crucial part of the diagnostic or interpretive exploration of the issues at stake for the client.

Warmth is crucial in intercultural counseling. The understandings and implications of being 'non-possessive' need to be examined within and between different social groups. Distancing, which we have indicated is a part of empathy, may be experienced as coldness by those particular cultural groups that have been socialized to value emotional expressiveness and intimacy as signs of care. Intercultural sensitivity is called for here. Through a genuine owning of one's cultural 'baggage,' one may be freed to examine one's responses and their appropriateness or otherwise in navigating the waters of any current counseling relationship.

GENUINENESS

Counseling relationships require a degree of openness and transparency which may not be evident in other professional encounters. Genuineness in counseling, sometimes referred to as *congruence*, means that the counselor offers the authentic openness of an honest humanity. It refers to the authenticity, as a goal as well as a means, by which a counselor remains an integrated person in the relationship. She or he is freely and deeply him/herself with no façade, 'phoney' mannerisms or professional role-playing.

The term congruence is used to stress that all aspects of the counselor's inner experience during the interview are freely admissible to awareness.

This is not to suggest that all inner feelings may therefore immediately be disclosed and 'dumped' onto the client. Instead, the counselor is aware of his or her feelings and, as appropriate, may self-disclose if that may assist the client's own self-disclosure and thus help in moving the relationship on.

A common experience in everyday life is that this characteristic is sensed. People seem to trust persons they sense are being what they are in open and transparent ways. By the same token people tend to be cautious about revealing themselves to people they perceive to be playing a role or relating from behind some form of mask.

The genuine counselor is spontaneous and expressive. Such counselors have no unacknowledged agenda remaining hidden and deeply buried away from the client. They avoid the defensiveness that is unable to cope with any negative attitudes to themselves on the part of their clients. If clients express negative feelings toward them, they do not engage in self-justifying, punitive or evasive behavior in response. Rather they seek to explore and understand such thoughts and feelings and to work with them in ways which may be useful in the therapeutic relationship. Genuineness often results in the appropriate and constructive application of self-disclosure, used as a means of furthering and freeing up the counseling process and not in a manipulative or exploitative fashion.

Self-disclosure may serve two purposes. First, modeling, by which clients are shown by example how they may disclose what is often difficult, painful or embarrassing. Second, it may help clients gain new perspectives on the issue at stake. Self-disclosure needs to be selective and focused and used sparingly, in order not to overwhelm or swamp the client. It is most appropriate if it helps the client open up and talk about themselves or else look more specifically at the issues they are presenting.

CONCRETENESS

Client and counselor are very often dealing with mixed emotions, muddled thinking and unfulfilling behavior. The interactions of these three can be as bewildering and baffling in living itself as they are in their communication within the counseling relationship. It is the task of counseling, as we have seen, to attempt to assist people find more satisfying responses to life. One 'ingredient' which the counselor may offer, is the endeavor to be concrete in communication.

Concreteness has to do with being definite, real and specific in what is said. The task is to avoid vagueness as much as is possible. At crucial points within the process, a counselor may seek to help clients avoid 'woolly emotionalizing'[7] of the issues. This may be done through modeling (stating more directly what might be the case) or sharpening (overstating the case or amplifying it), and in both these cases checking by asking for clarity and directness.

Concreteness aims at plain speech and direct communication in which messages are as clear, undistorted and uncontaminated as possible. In this sense, it has much in common with the characteristic often called *immediacy*, which we will be considering shortly.

CONFRONTATION

Confronting within counseling does not carry the connotation of attacking or challenging which the word often conveys. It is a responsible and caring activity. The intention is conveyed in the title of a book written by David Augsburger entitled *Caring Enough to Confront.* Counselors confront for at least two purposes. First, to draw attention to apparently unnoticed resources. A client may appear to be unaware of strengths that are evident in their personality or circumstances. If a counselor realizes the presence of such, it would be uncaring and insensitive not to draw the client's attention to possible sources of resolution or coping, which would otherwise be unrecognized. Second, to invite an examination of some form of behavior which may either be self-defeating or harmful to others (or both). The client's self-image and self-experience may be different from what the counselor is experiencing them to be. There may be discrepancies, distortions or contradictions in the life story being narrated or the body language accompanying it. There may be a tendency on the part of a client to blame others and never to own or accept responsibility for any part of a recurring problem. In either of such events, counselors draw on specific skills in drawing attention to the issues.

Confronting is most certainly not the first thing a counselor does on meeting a client. Most often issues needing attention only begin to emerge after many sessions together. It is part of the art of counseling to be able to gauge when it is appropriate to confront. There appears to be a 'critical period' before which it would be inappropriate and after which it would be ineffective to confront.

There are various ways in which a client may be confronted. Among them are the two that I have selected to illustrate the art. First, offering a plain description. Here the counselor describes in clear and concrete terms what s/he is beginning to see as self-defeating or counterproductive behavior or patterns of feeling or thought in the client. Second, the counselor encourages the client to act in the way they (the client) express a desire to and then to return to the next session for evaluation and discussion of their action and the feelings and consequences which went with it.

Confrontation is usually tentative, allowing for counselor misperception or misunderstanding. Egan describes these as counselor 'hunches.' But it always enables further exploration of ambiguous behavior.[8]

CONFIDENTIALITY

The principle of confidentiality undergirds all counseling activity. It is the principle which requires that personal information, revealed within a professional relationship, should not be divulged to any other person without the consent of the person who first offered it. By personal information is meant those aspects of a person's private life which are normally hidden from others, or shared only with trusted friends or relatives.

While this principle is generally accepted and adhered to in most counseling services, there are various ways in which moral, ethical, legal and statutory interprofessional regulations would require its reconsideration in cases where the safety of the client or of another person is at stake. It is beyond the scope of our consideration here to detail various strategies for responding to the situations where confidential material involves either criminal, harmful or potentially harmful behavior. Counselors are called upon to seek the well-being and safety of their clients. As such, they must follow legal and statutory regulations where the potential for harm is evident. This area, where the personal/private and public/statutory intersect, is an important area of attention and concern in various agencies within which counseling or counseling skills are employed.[9] Counselors must follow the guidelines of their accrediting, regulatory and supervisory bodies.

IMMEDIACY

Immediacy refers to the awareness within the counseling relationship of the actual 'here-and-now,' which is verbalized and examined. Egan refers to it as 'encouraging direct, mutual talk' or '*you-me*' talk (see Egan 1986, pp.231–238). Two forms of immediacy seem to be recognized. In the first, counselors discuss with clients the nature of their ongoing relationship in an open and frank exchange. The second pays attention to the specifics of 'what is going on between you and me just now.'

Immediacy requires awareness, know-how, communication skills and assertiveness. Counselors must be willing to monitor what is going on within the counseling relationship. Here supervision may be crucial, for it is within the counselors' supervision sessions that the opportunity to explore the nature of the counselor's relationship with the client may be given. In addition to this, however, here-and-now immediacy requires the ability to read cues within self and other, together with the assertiveness and communication skills to raise and explore issues, some of which may be quite difficult. Empathy, self-disclosure and confrontation skills are all called into play within this complex and difficult activity. Egan (1986) identifies at least seven situations in which immediacy activities are called for. These are when:

1. a session lacks direction

2. there is tension between counselor and client

3. trust seems to be an issue

4. there is social distance between counselor and client

5. dependency is interfering with the process

6. counterdependency is blocking the relationship

7. attraction is sidetracking counselor or client. Egan's conclusions on this and other 'skills of challenging' are instructive:

Immediacy is, of course, a means, not an end. The primary goal of the helping process is not to establish and enjoy relationships but to explore and work through problem situations. Immediacy, used effectively can…provide new perspectives on the counseling relationship and help client and counselor work more effectively together…what clients learn about themselves in their interactions with helpers can provide new perspectives on how they relate to people outside.' (Egan 1986, p.238)

Conclusion

Research among clients of psychotherapy has tended to suggest that the theoretical orientation of counselors and psychotherapists is not as significant as their ability to embody three major characteristics. David Howe (1993) has reported, very much in line with American research in the late 1960s, that it is the *genuineness,* secure trusting atmosphere, *empathy* and *warmth* which make all the difference in the counseling relationship. The 'therapeutic triad' of empathy, warmth and genuineness still remain the key characteristics of relevant and effective counseling.

Having examined the meaning, approaches and characteristics of counseling in general we shall now turn our attention to pastoral counseling.

Pastoral counseling

One of the interesting discussions which exercises the minds of some pastoral practitioners has to do with the distinctiveness or otherwise of 'pastoral counseling' from the general counseling activity we have been considering. In this respect, I can find six different ways in which the term 'pastoral' is understood and used in relation to counseling

1.   secular usage

2.   counseling by the ordained

3.   counseling with a religious frame of reference

4.   counseling offered within and by a community of faith

5.   christian counseling

6.   counseling for the whole person.

Secular usage

There is a secular usage of the term 'pastoral' in Britain, especially in educational circles. Here 'pastoral care' has to do with a concern for the personal welfare and well-being of persons one is in relation with or responsible for. In a useful survey of areas where rigorous, analytical, and systematic research and evaluation were necessary in pastoral care in education, Ribbins and Best (1985) presented the following model of the features of the environment within which pastoral care is to happen:

> Pastoral care is something which happens/should happen between *teacher and student*, interacting in the context of an institution called a *school* or *college* which has *four inter-related dimensions* (disciplinary/order, welfare/ pastoral, academic/curricular and administrative/organisational) and which is, itself, located in a wider *social, historical and cultural milieu*. (p.22)

In this sense, schoolteachers, tutors, school guidance and counseling officers, directors of studies, lecturers and special needs teachers have 'pastoral' responsibility for those they oversee. Four dimensions of such 'pastoral care' are identified as

- discipline and order
- welfare and personal well-being
- curriculum and academic achievement
- administration, e.g. registration, organization of activities.

These are clearly necessary in the development of persons who are to become self-sufficient members of society. It is instructive that the term 'pastoral' has been retained for these efforts within a highly secularized environment.

Counseling by the ordained

On the other extreme, and most commonly in the United States, pastoral counseling is understood to be that form of counseling which ordained and trained clergypersons offer. Howard Clinebell makes explicit what most American authors appear to take for granted when he defines pastoral counseling as 'the utilization *by clergy* [emphasis added] of counseling and psychotherapeutic methods to enable individuals, couples and families to handle their personal crises and problems in living constructively' (in Campbell 1987, p.198). In the US, ordination has been a prerequisite for accreditation as a pastoral counselor, although as Clyde Steckel (1985) reports, an increasing number of Clinical Pastoral Education centers are offering 'programs to educate laity as pastoral counselors.' Reform Rabbi

Robert Katz, in an informative and enlightening book, demonstrates the rich and varied heritage out of which Rabbis offer counsel to Jews. He writes:

> Rabbis often feel they have to choose between taking the role of *mocheach*, moral judge, or the role of *menachem*, giver of care, consoler. Some Rabbis avoid both, preferring the role of *talmid chacham*, or disciple of the wise, objective teacher and guide – an honored role in the history of the rabbinate. (Katz 1985, p.21)

Rabbi Katz is, nevertheless, very much aware of the trends in current social life and the increasing expectations, especially among American Jews, that rabbis will be counselors concerned with the inner life of the individual, family and community. 'Even those commandments, or *mitzvot*, concerned with visiting the sick and counseling the bereaved, which were traditionally incumbent on all Jews, are now seen as "rabbinical,"' he asserts (p.19). It is true to say that in the thinking of many people this understanding of 'pastoral' counseling seems the most obvious one. However, the situation is different in Britain in particular where 'pastoral counseling is practiced by as many (if not more) "lay" people as it is by ordained ministers' (Foskett and Jacobs 1989, p.252). This reality raises important questions about assumptions and presuppositions concerning the term.

Counseling with a religious frame of reference

Foskett and Jacobs (1989), writing from within a British context, are keen not to limit the variety of expression of pastoral counseling by too precise a definition of its nature and aims. They would describe it as 'counselling which takes place *within and around the religious context*'. (my italics). They do offer slightly more help with what this 'context' might mean when they explain that they use the term 'religious' in an inclusive sense which reflects the interests not only of Jews and Christians but also of those who belong to no church 'but who consider matters of faith and ultimate concern as of relevance to them and their clients.' As such, pastoral counseling 'also refers to counseling which takes religious problems seriously, and which is informed by the counselor's concern for ultimate values and meanings – religion in its widest sense.' Religion is not the exclusive concern but rather is seen as relevant in as much as a client may see it as such.

Counseling offered within and by a community of faith

One of the sharp criticisms of pastoral counseling for which the late R.A. Lambourne of Birmingham is well known is of its 'individualism.' He argued for a more corporate conceptualization of pastoral counseling, seeing it as 'the Church growing towards perfection (towards maturity) as, taught by God, it learns in the service of God and neighbour what it must do to be saved' (Lambourne 1969/1995, p.73). Lambourne's concerns are echoed in the work of American pastoral theologian E.E. Thornton, who recognizes that the individual or dyadic concentration of pastoral counseling is 'a symptom, not the cause' of a wider cultural malaise in which the institutionalized church fully shares – namely the absence of community (Thornton 1987).

Christian counseling

From the evangelical Christian persuasion has emerged an approach to counseling which has been described as 'Christian counseling'. While evangelicals have tended not to use the term 'pastoral' to convey their counseling practice, perhaps in this way distinguishing themselves from the more liberal branches of Christianity, many appreciate the value of psychological research and seek to integrate that with what is the heart of 'Christian' counseling, namely the Bible. Indeed, evangelical Christian counselors seek to base their counsel on a particular reading and interpretation of the Bible that is based on an experience of salvation through personal faith in Jesus Christ. This experience is the central theological and interpretive framework in relation to which people's responses to the exigencies of life are explored.

The main differences between evangelical Christian counselors have to do with the degree to which they are prepared to make use of 'secular' psychological knowledge in relation to their biblical and doctrinal framework. On one extreme, American Jay E. Adams (1970) claims that there is no need for *any* psychology whatsoever.[10] On the other hand, there is Gary R. Collins, also an American, who holds a PhD in clinical psychology from Purdue University. He has proposed a rebuilding of psychology on the theistic premise that 'God exists and is the source of all truth' (Collins 1977, p.118; see especially pp.115–133). Collins has written extensively on 'Christian counseling' and has been a major source of teaching and practice in this area (see e.g. Collins 1990). Similarly, and also very influential among British evangelicals would be American Larry Crabb, also a holder of a PhD in clinical psychology (from the University of Illinois). Crabb prefers the term 'biblical counseling' and, in place of a simplistic 'witch-hunting' Christianity *and* a psychology which has no time for 'sin,' he seeks to offer

> a solidly biblical approach to counseling, one which draws from secular psychology without betraying its Scriptural premise, one which realistically faces the deep (and not so deep) problems of people and honestly evaluates its success in dealing with them, and, most importantly, one which clings passionately and unswervingly to belief in an inerrant Bible and an all-sufficient Christ. (Crabb 1976, p.18)

In Britain, Selwyn Hughes, founder of the Crusade for World Revival housed, since 1983, in Waverley Abbey House (Farnham, Surrey), is perhaps the most well-known exponent of biblical counseling (see Hughes 1981).

A comprehensive and more scholarly and detailed treatment of counseling and psychotherapy from an evangelical perspective has come from British counselor and medical practitioner Roger Hurding. Hurding (1985) presents a historical survey of the field that is both wide and broad. Essentially, he, like Collins, Crabb and Hughes, offers an integrationist view while maintaining the supremacy of 'scriptural insight' (see also Hurding 1992).

Most recently, a socially critical, philosophically and theologically more informed approach has been offered which arises from a similarly evangelical standpoint. Bridger and Atkinson (1994) argue for the importance of relating a person's psychological context to their social context. They continue:

> Neither psychological nor social contexts can be divorced from philosophy and theology. These are fundamental to human beings. The distinctive task of the Christian counsellor is to enable a counsellee to face critical questions with theological as well as psychological resources (p.21)

A discernible feature in the development of Christian counseling, therefore, is a growth in the breadth of coverage of subject area without loss of a basic commitment to the centrality of a particular reading of scripture. This was foreshadowed in the voluminous and prolific work of the late British psychiatrist, medical missionary, and latterly charismatic Christian, Frank Lake. Lake founded the Clinical Theology Association in Britain, which has provided pastoral counseling training in groups for large numbers of clergy, ministers and laypersons. Lake, a true pioneer who fearlessly launched into uncharted waters, introduced his work[11] in his *magnum opus Clinical Theology*, by describing 'clinical theology' as

> substantially theology, putting faith, ultimately, not in human wisdom but in the love and power of God, yet meticulously observant of the sound practice of psychiatry and psychotherapy, with the restraints upon religious (or anti-religious) influencing which are properly implicit in them. (Lake 1966, p.*xii*)

An interesting theological difference from the classical evangelical position is present in Lake's work and emerges even within this brief quotation. Lake's faith is not so much in the 'written word' as it is in 'the love and power of God.' The Clinical Theology Association, currently known as the Bridge Foundation, serves as one of the major bridging agencies between those who would prefer to speak of 'Christian Counselling' and those who name their practice 'pastoral counselling'.

Counseling for the whole person

A way of understanding pastoral counseling, which enters into the debate about the difference between 'religion' and 'spirituality' in an important manner, has been suggested by Chris R. Schlauch. This is the way Schlauch (1985) envisages pastoral counseling:

> Counseling for the whole person, as an individual as well as part of a family and social unit, and as a whole person, body, mind and spirit, but with particular reference to the person's psychological, ethical and theological frames of reference. (Schlach 1985, p.223)

The viewing of a pastoral concern as being a concern for the whole person is what distinguishes this understanding from others that appear to have a particular 'religious' concern. Schlauch himself does not entirely escape this focus in that in the latter part of his description he does indicate a particular reference point for pastoral counseling. However, this reference is in effect quite vague – the person's 'psychological, ethical and theological frames of reference.' The most important part of his contribution, in my view, lies in the holistic understanding offered.

This sense of holism is conveyed in a work on the nursing concept of spiritual care, which raises the question whether spiritual care concerns being 'wholly responsible for a part, or partly responsible for a whole' (Mayer 1989). Many of the forms of pastoral counseling we have surveyed could be described as 'wholly responsible for a part,' namely the religious part. A holistic understanding, on the other hand, emphasizes 'being partly responsible for the whole.' What this means is that, pastoral counselors work alongside others in seeking the total well-being of all persons. This totality includes individual bodies, minds and spirits, families and other social units. It also brings psychological, social, ethical and theological perspectives to bear upon all its concerns.

Critique of counseling

From within the ranks of psychotherapists has arisen a sharp, healthy debate and criticism of the theory and practice of psychotherapy and as such, counseling. Dryden and Feltham (1992) have recently done the service of editing a collection of essays, responses and rebuttals from eight practitioners and consumers of therapy. Among the issues discussed in this collection are: the inadequacy of research validating the outcomes of psychotherapy (Kline); the possibility that psychotherapy is no more effective than no treatment at all (Eysenck); consumers' experience of therapy as harmful (Eysenck, Sutherland, Mair, Masson); the mystically self-protective nature of psychotherapy and its culture (Gellner); the pretentiousness of therapists' explanations (Mair); the widespread personal fallibility and exploitativeness of therapists (Masson);[12] psychotherapy's anachronistic detachment from new models (Edwards); and psychological reductionism and political lethargy which weaken any political credibility therapy might have (Pilgrim). To this striking list, the editors add a number of other concerns. First, the fissiparous nature of the field of psychotherapy with schools breaking up into splinter groups, feuds between traditionalists and reformers, purists and eclectics, together with a plethora of brands of therapy and counseling on offer. Second, an apparent aphilosophical, fiercely pragmatic stance adopted by some practitioners with little or no concern for epistemological questions concerning how we are sure about what we claim to know. Third, the cult-like nature of the field with 'trainees (and masters!) congregating around institutes, workshops and charismatic leaders' (Dryden and Feltham 1992, p.259). Fourth, 'most therapy in practice is endemically middle-class and ethnocentric. It is only just beginning to react adequately to the realities of the socio-economic position of women and ethnic, and other, minorities' (p.260).

Finally, in Dryden and Feltham's book, questions are raised concerning accountability, credibility and the extent to which therapists are any better models of healthy parenting than others. The parallels here with developments in religion and religious groups are quite remarkable.

Clearly, where counseling operates as the model for pastoral care these kinds of issues and concerns are relevant. They go to the very heart of the theory and practice of the art of 'talking cures' as it has been developed in the twentieth century Western world. The question that follows on immediately from these considerations has to do with pastoral counseling. What issues and concerns have been raised about the practice of pastoral counseling?

There are at least four principal areas in which a critique of pastoral counseling has been made. These are its *psychological reductionism, sociopolitical apathy, theological weakness* and *individualism.*

On psychological reductionism, of the various writers and practitioners who have raised the concern, two should suffice to make the point. Pattison (1986) has argued that pastoral counselors have preferred the analytical tools of outdated psychological theorists to any theological or social analysis of the present day experiences of their clients. Oden has also demonstrated conclusively 'that contemporary psychotherapists are far more inwardly important and objectively authoritative for pastoral counseling today than are the writers of classical Christian pastoral care' (Oden 1984, p.32).

On sociopolitical apathy, the arguments marshalled by Pilgrim (1992) in critique of psychotherapy are paralleled eloquently and clearly in the works of Pattison (1993) and Leech (1992) on the side of pastoral care and counseling. Michael Wilson (1988) brings the point of the criticism to a sharp focus when he writes: 'You cannot help people fully unless you also do something about the situation which makes them what they are' (p.21).

Issues of economic and social power, marginalization, access and social control have a direct bearing on the personal and emotional well-being of people in any society. That pastoral counselors, in the same way as other counselors in the Western world, have not in general included such considerations in their theory or practice is unfortunate.

Of the theological weakness of pastoral counseling much has been written. From the virulent writings of Lambourne in the 1960s, in which he charged the growing pastoral counseling movement with replacing the symbols of Christian faith with psychotherapeutic ones, changing theology into anthropology and the idolatrous turning of the relationship between counselor and client into 'God' (see especially Lambourne 1969/1995), to Leroy Howe's (1995) attempt to provide a theology for Christian pastoral counselors,[13] this fundamental weakness is acknowledged. It is one thing to make the criticism, it is quite another to actually provide a response to it. It is gratifying to observe that some Christian pastoral counselors are responding to this challenge (e.g. Poling 1991, especially pp.153–173).[14]

Finally, the charge of individualism has been leveled by many, including Lambourne, Mathers, Thornton, Pattison, Guthrie and Dyson.[15] It is perhaps in the nature of things that Western forms of pastoral counseling have stressed the intrapsychic, inner lives of hurting people as the focus of therapy. In cultural settings where human persons are defined more in communal and interpersonal terms, forms of counseling which have developed, even where they have been in interaction with Western ideas, have managed to retain the sense of 'belonging to a whole' within their therapeutic focus. A relevant example is the 'African Christian Palaver' about which Kasonga (1994) has recently written.

This brings us to the end of our considerations of what might be called a particularly Western approach to pastoral care. As we have seen whether counseling is used as a form of pastoral care or 'pastoral counseling' is offered from a particular religious standpoint, it is true to say that to a large extent the assumptions, anthropological and cultural presuppositions as well as the forms of practice entailed, are amenable to Western industrialized society. In the next chapter, we shall be considering a form of pastoral care which appears to characterize other cultures and which, taken together with counseling, has the potential to assist in the development of 'holistic communities in which all people can live humane lives.'

Notes

1. For two useful books offering exercises in listening skills see Michael Jacobs' *Still Small Voice: An Introduction to Pastoral Counselling* (SPCK, 1982) and *Swift To Hear* (SPCK, 1985).

2. The date, I am sure, accounts for the sexist language. Bonhoeffer's piece in the section of Chapter 4 headed 'The Ministry of Listening' is essential reading for all ministers.

3. There are very many ways in which religious and philosophical traditions seek to account for evil in humanity and the world.

4. For a very useful summary of relevant research which shows the importance of Black perspectives, see Robinson (1995, pp.29–45).

5. For a discussion of the relevance of nonverbal cues in 'cross-cultural counseling,' see Sue and Sue(1990, pp.49–74). Though I have problems with the basic thesis and the presentation of the material in this book, which in my view unavoidably encourages stereotypical thinking, it offers some useful insights.

6. For work within a British context, see Lago and Thompson (1989).

7. The expression is from Carkhuff (1969).

8. For a very useful and concise discussion, see Egan (1986, pp.219–228).

9. For a concise and very useful consideration of confidentiality, boudaries and supervision in counseling relevant to these concerns, see Lyall (1996, pp.56–79).

10. In effect, Adams advocates a neo-behaviorism in which particular 'sinful' behaviors are targeted for change through the use of learning-theory-based methods derived from the scriptures.

11. For a very accessible introduction to Frank Lake's work, see Christian (1991). A more recent evaluation of the formative years is Ross (1994).

12. For a fuller documentation of this, see Masson (1989).

13. Howe (1995) writes, 'pastoral counseling at its best proceeds from an informed faith sustained by involvement in a community whose ministry to its members and in the world flows naturally from continuous theological reflection' (p.11).

14. Also worth mentioning, among others, are the works of Don Browning, John Patton, Thomas Oden and Rebecca Chopp.

15. For a selection of papers from each of these authors, see Jacobs (1987).

CHAPTER 6

Liberation as Pastoral Praxis

A theme that has challenged the theory and practice of pastoral care in many parts of the so-called Third World is that of liberation. Peruvian Catholic priest Gustavo Gutiérrez offered the first formal outlines of liberation theology at a pastoral conference in Chimbote, Peru, in July 1968. At about the same time, Brazilian protestant Rubem Alves presented a doctoral thesis to Princeton Theological Seminary, which was later published under the title *A Theology of Human Hope* (Alves 1969). It is significant that African American theologian James Cone, at this very time, presented his revolutionary theological reflections on the Black power movement (Cone 1969).

Gutiérrez's work, which appeared in book form in Lima in December 1971 and was later published in English (Gutiérrez 1974), was the first full-blown systematic discussion of the term 'liberation theology,' which he had coined. *A Theology of Liberation* was the tip of an iceberg, for it articulated and formalized thinking which characterized a number of religious and social movements across the globe. The women's liberation movement, the civil rights and Black power movements and revolutionary movements in Central and South America were all expressing their opposition to sexual, racial, class and sociopolitical oppression.

What Gutiérrez proposed was not simply another theology of 'so-and-so,' but rather a radically different way of engaging in the task of theology. As has been borne out by the influence this new methodology has had among groups of people across the world, the new liberation theology was both revolutionary and relevant. Since the early 1970s, Latin American liberation theology has been associated with Black theology, both in the United States and South Africa, and feminist theologies, which also understand themselves as liberation theologies. Movements like *Minjung* theology in South Korea, *Dalit* theology in India and womanist theology among women in the African diaspora, bear the imprint of the theological method articulated by the South Americans. With the establishment of the Ecumenical Association of Third World Theologians (EATWOT) in 1976, liberation theology has come to be shaped as a major theological expression of the 'Third World.'[1] There is a lively and healthy debate within EATWOT about the relative merits and demerits of the Latin American emphases in the different Asian and African contexts, to which I shall refer at the appropriate points in this discussion.

In this chapter, my concern is to examine the relevance of the methodology of liberation theology for the theory and practice of pastoral care. In order to do this I shall begin by outlining the essentials of the method, with reference to its outworkings among some marginalized groups, pointing out some of the critical observations that have emerged from other Third World settings. This will be no more than a sketch that will seek to identify the core elements, rather than an extensive treatment – of which there are many available, some not very accessible because of language and style of writing. In the final analysis, I shall inquire about the extent to which liberation theology provides an adequate method for engaging in and reflecting upon pastoral care.

Core elements in liberation theology

Liberation theology essentially offers a *standpoint* and *three reflective procedures* for achieving the goal of the liberation of the oppressed. The standpoint is 'a prior political and ethical option in the light of the gospel, *for the poor.*' Liberation theology is contextual. It is theology that is engaged in from a position that has been identified, chosen and clearly stated. The theologian first commits him or herself to being in a particular place and engaging with others in work that aims at liberating the oppressed. The context of liberation theology is a particular oppressed community that is 'conscientized' and galvanized into collective reflection and action. As Leonardo Boff (Boff and Boff 1987) puts it, 'it is a matter of trying to live the commitment of faith: in our case, to participate in some way in the process of liberation, to be committed to the oppressed' (p.22).

This stance has been described as the preliminary prerequisite for any liberation theology. It has also been called a pre-theological first step in the process. Hence, for any liberation theology to be undertaken, it is the theologian who must first become different. Leonardo and Clodovis Boff indicate that at this point it is not so much the method, as the 'person' that is at stake.

Rather than introducing a new theological method, liberation theology is a new way of being a theologian. Theology is always a second step; the first is the 'faith that makes its power felt through love' (Galations 5:6). Theology (not the theologian) comes afterward; liberating practice first (Boff and Boff 1987).

The theologian begins from a position of being immersed in the experiences of poverty, marginalization and oppression. It is from this position that s/he tries to understand and articulate the faith. The theology of liberation begins with a concern for the liberation of the poor, and as such tries to articulate a reading of reality and faith 'through the eyes of the poor.' Liberation theologians have chosen the option of evaluating social reality from the viewpoint of the poor, of engaging in theological reflection on the basis of the experiences of poverty and marginalization, and of acting for the liberation of the poor. This option determines the *social* context from where the theologian engages in theology. In this way, much store is set by the social location of the participants in any theological or redemptive endeavor. To what extent do they participate in the experiences they describe and reflect on? How representative are they of the issues they discuss?

Leonardo and Clodovis Boff argue that personal contact is necessary if one is to acquire the required sensitivity. They identify three types of commitment to and identification with the poor. On one level, contact is more or less restricted to visits, meetings and consultative or pastoral contact. On a second level, there would be alternating periods of research, teaching and writing with periods of practical work with the poor. 'The third level is that of those who live *permanently* with the people, making their home among the people, living and working alongside the people' (Boff and Boff 1987, p.23).

This basic framework has been extended and adapted by attempts to answer questions like: Who are the poor? Who speaks for the poor? Who has the power and control in the articulation of the experiences of the poor? Who selects what is relevant? Who benefits from the way things are done? Who is excluded? Who is marginalized? A fourth level is therefore discernible in the 'first step' of those who would describe their work as liberative. At this level, it is the poor, marginalized or oppressed who speak for themselves, on their own terms and in their own chosen manner. An important example of this latter point can be found in *womanism*, in which Black women who suffer the 'multiple jeopardy' of being oppressed on grounds of gender, race, color and socio-economic class, have found their own voice (see Grant 1989).

This 'option for the poor' also determines the epistemological context (the manner in which the theologian 'does' theology), which I shall be discussing when I present the reflective procedures of a theology of liberation. The standpoint of liberation theology has been found useful for various types of contextual theology relevant to pastoral care. Pattison writes about its effects in psychiatric hospital chaplaincy.[2] The Archbishop of Canterbury's Commission on Urban Priority Areas (1985) adopted a similar approach to their work on deprived inner-city areas of the United Kingdom. James Harris (1991) reflects very usefully on the approach within the Black church in the United States. Archbishop Desmond Tutu (1984), Allan Boesak (1978) and other Black South Africans (e.g. Moore 1973; Mosala 1989) have articulated it from within their own context as has Biblical scholar Itumeleng Mosala with reference to interpreting the Bible in South Africa. Laurie Green (1990) employed this standpoint and approach in formulating a 'pastoral cycle' based on his work with parishioners in Birmingham and as Director of the Aston Training Scheme, a national ordination course in Britain.

The three reflective procedures followed in liberation theology are:

- social analysis
- hermeneutical analysis
- the praxis orientation.

Social analysis

In contrast both to classical Western theology, which has tended to use the disciplines of philosophy as its main analytical tools, and to pastoral care, which, as we have seen, borrows heavily from psychology, liberation theology uses the social sciences as major sources for an understanding of the structures of poverty. Basically, the Latin American originators of liberation theology saw socio-economic poverty as the fundamental expression of oppression and sought to find what its causes were. Three main explanations of the causes of poverty were available within social scientific analysis. First, an *individualist* explanation that attributed poverty to laziness or ignorance. The solution to poverty on this understanding was aid either on a personal almsgiving basis or through national fund-raising efforts. On such a view the poor are objects of pity and charity. Second, there was a *bourgeois* explanation, which saw the causes of poverty lying in economic and social backwardness. The sociopolitical solution put forward was a kind of 'trickle-down effect' in which there was a gradual improvement of the existing system through schemes of wealth creation. Improved technology and loans would help to pull the backward nations and social groups up and thus to slowly advance their economic position. Here, the poor are passive objects of actions taken by others. Third, a *dialectical* explanation in which poverty is seen as a result of oppression. Poverty in this model is an integral part of the structure of the capitalist economic organization of society. Here the many – who only have their labor to sell – are exploited by the few – who own the means of production and distribution. Society is a collective and conflictual organism in which the rich exploit the poor in order to keep their positions of affluence and control. The way out is a revolutionary transformation of the very basis of the economic and social system. The poor, in this rendering, are the 'subjects and agents' of their own liberation.

Latin American liberation theologians found the dialectical explanation most useful in their quest to understand and change the situation of the masses of their people. This explanation is, of course, the Marxist one. Marx developed his tools of analysis at the height of the European industrial revolution and the growth of the capitalist mode of production and distribution. Regardless of how one views Marx, his analysis of the capitalist mode of production, of the tensions between those who own the means of production and those who labor for the owners, and of surplus value and profit, cannot be ignored. As Cornel West (1981) has argued, 'some form of Marxist analysis is indispensable to understand the international economic order, capitalist societies and the perpetuation and preservation of gross inequalities and injustices in those societies' (p.255).

A necessary part of social analysis is the recognition of political and historical processes. Any attempt to respond to the question 'Why are some people poor?' must address issues of colonialism, expansionism, neo-colonialism and industrialization. The poor are not only focused upon in their current situation, but as a product of a historical process of plunder and exploitation. Moreover, socio-economic poverty is seen not so much as caused by personal or familial distortions, but rather as a structural and societal phenomenon requiring 'historico-structural' analysis and response.

The utilization of a Marxist analysis of history and society is the point on which liberation theologians have been most severely criticized. The most frequently cited issue in this regard is the Marxist critique of religion. Liberation theologians are accused of not taking Marx's critique of religion seriously enough. Liberation theologians, in turn, have offered rebuttals of this criticism. The clearest recent statement I have come across is that offered by Leonardo and Clodovis Boff. I think it is worth quoting in full:

> In liberation theology, Marxism is never treated as a subject on its own but always *from and in relation to the poor*. Placing themselves firmly on the side of the poor, liberation theologians ask Marx: 'What can you tell us about the situation of poverty and ways of overcoming it?' Here Marxists are submitted to the judgment of the poor and their cause, and not the other way around. Therefore, liberation theology uses Marxism purely as an *instrument*. It does not venerate it as it venerates the gospel. (Boff and Boff 1987, p.28)

According to the Boff brothers then, liberation theologians borrow from Marxism particular questions, methods and analyses that have proved fruitful in understanding the world of the oppressed. These include the importance of economic factors, attention to class struggle, and the mystifying power of ideologies, including religious ones. They go on to argue that 'liberation theology, therefore, maintains a decidedly critical stance in relation to Marxism… This being so, Marxist materialism and atheism do not even constitute a temptation for liberation theologians' (Boff and Boff 1987, p.28).

The exclusive focus on socio-economic poverty in the early years of Latin American liberation theology has been criticized widely, not least within the meetings of EATWOT. Asian and African theologians have pointed out the failure of the South American theologians to pay attention to ethnic oppression in which the native Amerindians and black Latin Americans have been caught. These indigenous people have been absent from South American liberation theology. Women from all over the world clearly articulate their oppressed status while women of color show how discriminated against they have been by white women. African, Asian and minority-American theologians, have called for a greater emphasis on sociocultural analyses which emphasize and examine racial and cultural oppression.

Social analysis then, when applied in different societies and cultures in different parts of the world, yields different results. What is increasingly being realized is the multiplicity of oppression and the interconnectedness of 'multiple oppressions' experienced by particular people. Various forms of oppression are present to different degrees in all societies. Oppression may be the result of social, economic, political, racial, gender, class, age, religious or cultural difference. Various combinations of these may be present in the experience of particular groups of people. The Boff brothers acknowledge that 'the poor are additionally oppressed when, beside being poor, they are also black, indigenous, women or old' (Boff and Boff 1987, p.30).

In an incisive paper, reflecting on the December 1986 EATWOT meeting held in Oaxtepec, Mexico, the then General Secretary of the South African Council of Churches, Frank Chikane, while showing the need for a Marxist social analysis, demonstrated the inadequacy of such an analysis in 'dealing with religio-cultural realities' in some parts of the Third World. Chikane writes:

> To achieve this level of consciousness and sensitivity we need to use all effective tools of analysis for all these forms of oppression. The tools of Third World liberation theologies must, therefore, include both the religio-cultural and socio-economic and political perspective. We must use both the religio-cultural and Marxist tools of analysis... integrating these two models...into a comprehensive social analysis which is capable of capturing any level or form of oppression in our societies and in the world at large. (Chikane 1990, p.166)

Hermeneutical analysis

The second stage in liberation theology is more formally theological. In the first stage the liberation theologian has gone some way toward an understanding of the real situation of the oppressed. At this second stage, the liberation theologian asks the question, 'What has the word of God to say about this?' Without the prior option for the poor and the social analysis that has been engaged in, this kind of question could court the disastrous conventional responses and 'pat answers' against which liberation theology protests. Uruguayan theologian Juan Luis Segundo offers perhaps the most helpful explanation of the hermeneutical phase of liberation theology (see Segundo 1976, especially Chapter 1).

Segundo (1976) argues that since Christianity is a *biblical* religion, Christian theologians have to keep going back to 'its book' and reinterpreting it. He is convinced, however, that the task is not simply one of going back to the past and producing abstract, ahistorical theories, which are then applied to the people of today. Instead the liberation theologian 'feels compelled at every step to combine the disciplines that open up the past with the disciplines that help to explain the present' (p.8). Segundo calls the method of relating past and present in dealing with the word of God, the *hermeneutic circle*, which he explains is

> the continuing change in our interpretation of the Bible that is dictated by the continuing changes in our present-day reality, both individual and societal... And the circular nature of this interpretation stems from the fact that each new reality obliges us to interpret the word of God afresh, to change reality accordingly, and then to go back and reinterpret the word of God again, and so on. (p.8)

Segundo argues that if customary interpretations are not questioned and changed, then contemporary problems will 'go unanswered, or worse, they will receive old, conservative, unserviceable answers' (p.9).

Clodovis Boff further seeks to clarify the hermeneutic orientation of liberation theology by referring to it as a *relationship of relationships*. On the one hand, there is the relationship between scripture and its context (Segundo's 'past'). On the other hand, there is the relationship between ourselves and our socio-economic and political context (Segundo's 'present'). Boff contends that what is vital is the 'spirit' or relationship that may exist between these two relationships.

We need not, then, look for formulas to 'copy' or techniques to 'apply' from scripture. What scripture will offer us are rather things like orientations, models, types, directives, principles, inspirations – elements permitting us to acquire, on our own initiative, a 'hermeneutic competency.' Thus we achieve the capacity to judge – on our own initiative, in our own right – 'according to the mind of Christ' or 'according to the Spirit,' the new, unpredictable situations with which we are continually confronted. The Christian writings offer us not a *what*, but a *how* – a manner, a style, a spirit (Boff 1987). These South American hermeneutical approaches, in the main, accept the scriptures as given and seek new ways to work with them in the current oppressive contexts of the world.

There are other approaches from 'the margins' (see Sugirtharajah 1995) that are more critical of the sources as given. Some feminist perspectives, for example, raise questions about the texts themselves as received, pointing out their sexist, exclusivist and oppressive nature for women (Trible 1992).

The most radical critique of the whole Christian hermeneutic exercise comes from the multi-religious societies of Asia, where scriptural religions abound. Sugirtharajah (1993) reminds us that for more than four thousand years different faith communities in Asia have drawn inspiration from a wide variety of scriptural texts. He refers to the *Upanishads*, the *Brahma Sutras* and the *Bhagavadgita* – the triple canon of Hindus, the *Pali* canon of Buddhists and the *Agamas* of Jains, which have been investigated and interpreted long before the advent of Western Christianity. In such a religiously complex context, Sugirtharajah points out two responses to the Bible. One he terms 'the non-use' and the other 'the re-use' of the Bible. Examples of the former include Sadhu Sundar Singh, Pandipedi Chenchiah and more recently M. M. Thomas, who sought 'the raw fact of Christ' (the famous phrase of Chenchiah) unmediated through text, creed or sacrament. Of the latter, Sugirtharajah examines the work of I. Vempeny from India, well-known Taiwanese theologian C-S. Song and Archie Lee Chi Chung from Hong Kong. Vempeny and others have used texts from Hindu or Buddhist sources, on the one hand to present aspects of the social teaching of Jesus to Hindus, and on the other hand to remind Christians of forgotten aspects of Christian teaching. C-S. Song 'pioneered the method of creatively juxtaposing myths, stories and legends with biblical narratives and of constantly going beyond the written word to the symbolic meaning' (Sugirtharajah 1993, p.59).

Among the important doors that the hermeneutic circle of liberation theology seems to have opened for liberation theologians has been the possibility with some degree of flexibility, to allow texts to interact with people in their everyday social contexts. The result has been an enhanced dialectical relationship between social analysis and the 'texts and teachings' of different faith communities.

The praxis orientation

Liberation theology begins with action and ends with action. It seeks to be a militant, committed and liberating theology. The 'action' involved however, is not 'mindless.' The term 'praxis' is used to convey the sense of constant interaction between *action* and *reflection*. Boff and Boff (1987) identify three levels at which liberation theology operates. These are the professional, the pastoral and the popular. In theological institutes, universities and seminaries, professional liberation theologians produce conference papers, books, articles and seminar papers. Pastoral ministers offer sermons, talks, pastoral care, counseling and community action from their bases in churches, pastoral institutes and centers within the communities. At the popular level, base communities, Bible study groups and community action groups meet to study, reflect, attend training courses and engage in strategically planned political action in quest of better socio-economic conditions and a more just society.

The goal of liberation theology is not the production of more adequate theory or clearer statement of belief. It is right action for change. This is the *orthopraxis* that, instead of *orthodoxy*, is seen as crucial for theological engagement. However, it is recognized that the process of acting can be extremely complex. In its Roman Catholic formulation, liberation theologians have tended to see professional theologians (clergy) as pointing 'only to broad lines of action.' It is the task of pastor-theologians and, more especially, the popular theologian (laity) to 'go deeply into the particular course to be followed in a specific case.' In both these cases such action may be collective. Protestant liberation theologians would criticize this sharp division of labor between clergy and laity as hierachical, dualistic, unwittingly perpetuating the false theory/practice division and potentially damaging to effective communal action.

Action is seen as necessarily involving various steps and stages. It is necessary to decide the course of action on the basis of reasonable and careful appreciation of all the circumstances involved. It is important to attempt to anticipate the consequences and effects of the proposed action.

It is crucial to follow a planned strategy and program of action that has an inbuilt evaluative and reflective phase. Liberation theologians would argue that much more may be learnt from actual involvement in action than from theory alone. As such, a critical and dialectical relationship is sought between action and reflection.

Liberation theology and pastoral care

One of the ongoing concerns of practitioners of pastoral care, and of pastoral theologians, has been the quest for appropriate methodologies and theoretical frames that will enable more serious engagement between theory and practice, theology and pastoral care. This search, it is true to say, is discernible in almost any part of the world to which one may turn. I shall be arguing here that in a critical appropriation of the methodologies of liberation theology, may lie one suitable response to this quest. I wish also, on the basis of 20 years of experiencing and teaching intercultural pastoral care in West Africa and Britain, to suggest the intercultural value of the methodology adopted by liberation theologians.

There are four areas of engagement between liberation theology and pastoral care that I shall now explore:

- concrete experience
- social analysis
- hermeneutical analysis
- the pastoral praxis of liberation.

The starting place – concrete experience

As we have seen, liberation theologians begin from the concrete experience of the poor. Similarly, practitioners of pastoral care engage in 'helping activities' with actual people in real situations. There would therefore appear to be much ground for dialogue between them. However, pastoral caregivers have tended to emphasize the personal, intimate small group or developmental experiences that have influenced or shaped people for good or ill. Liberation theologians, on the other hand, have focused upon social and political systems that have been oppressive of social groups. These are very different readings of the human situation and of the loci of therapeutic or transformative focus. However, they are the two sides of one coin.

The feminist maxim 'the personal is political' is instructive here. What is termed 'personal' often has tremendous political ramifications. What happens to individual children within the personal, small-group space of 'the family' may have lasting psychosocial and indeed political repercussions. Political philosophies which make a sharp division between the private and the public often do so for economic reasons seeking to shift the burden of provision from the government onto the shoulders of families and individuals. Such approaches are then termed 'competitive,' permitting individual choice and market forces to operate to the benefit of individuals. Sight is lost of those who, for various social and historical reasons, have been rendered unable to 'compete.' At this point, the corollary of the saying is equally illuminating – 'the political is personal.' Decisions made in the boardrooms of power may result in illness, loss of psychological balance, family breakdown and intolerable personal distress. Korean woman theologian Chung Hyun Kyung, who stirred the 1991 World Council of Churches Assembly in Canberra with a spectacular liturgical presentation of Asian women's Christianity, puts it vividly:

> Han[3] is the most prevalent feeling among Korean people, who have been violated throughout their history by the surrounding powerful countries. This feeling arises from a sense of impasse. Often Korean people, especially the poor and women, have not had any access to public channels through which they can challenge the injustices done to them. They have long been silenced by physical and psychological intimidation and actual bodily violence by the oppressor. When there is no place where they can express their true selves, their true feelings, the oppressed become 'stuck' inside. This unexpressed anger and resentment stemming from social powerlessness forms a 'lump' in their spirit. This lump often leads to a lump in the body, by which I mean the oppressed often disintegrate bodily as well as psychologically. (Chung 1991, p.42)

A starting point that may bring together the approaches of pastoral caregivers and liberation theologians would require a valuing of both. This should be possible because both seek to be located in the concrete experiences of the suffering, the poor and the oppressed. Both need to be present empathically in the experience of those who suffer. Both need to *see* clearly the totality of the experience of the people they work with. Both participate in a reality which transcends the personal as well as the sociopolitical. Both must allow those who suffer the complete freedom to express, in their own way, the 'length and breadth and height and depth' of their experience. Pastoral practitioners need visions of breadth; liberation theologians need revelations of depth. Both need each other's view.

From an intercultural perspective this commitment to concrete experience is essential. For intercultural pastoral care to be *liberative* it must be *inductive, collective* and *inclusive*. An example of this way of working comes from Asian women's theological consultations, as reported by Chung Hyun Kyung. These begin with the embodied truth of women's 'storytelling.' 'Educated middle-class women theologians are committed to inviting or visiting poor farmers, factory workers, slum dwellers, dowry victims and prostitutes and listening to their life stories' Chung 1991, p.104). Women talk about their concrete, historical life experience. Kim Young Bok refers to this storytelling as 'socio-biography' in which listeners hear, not cold data, but actual people's suffering, crying, longing and survival strategies. Chung writes: 'It is embodied historiography. Poor women's socio-biography is 'holistic, multidimensional and complex,' because it deals with the whole person and not some single aspect of personhood' (p.105).

Listening is a skill which, as we have seen, pastoral caregivers and counselors cannot do without. Interpathic listening would enable listeners to enter into the real-life, human experiences of people who struggle to recover their humanity in situations of oppression in all communities in the world.

This standpoint could guard against the overgeneralization that is a temptation of culturalists. It permits stereotypes to be challenged by the concrete experiences of living people – a crucial task in an intercultural approach. Examples of this can be found within women's experience. African American women have challenged the situation where their experience is subsumed, and therefore effectively excluded, by white feminists claiming to speak for all women. Womanists are not simply 'Black *feminists*' (see hooks 1981; Lorde 1984). In fact, in slavery white women were as oppressive of black women as were black men, if not more so (Grant 1989). Susan Thistlewaite (1990), a white feminist theologian acknowledges: 'White feminist theology is racist because it has assumed the prerogative of naming the world for black women on the basis of white women's definitions of experience' (p.101).

The power to define one's own experience on one's own terms is a vital part of liberation. As such, African American women have embarked on the task of articulating their own experience in the face of sexism from males – both white and black, racism from white women and classism from without and within their ranks. Issues of colorism (the lighter the better) and ageism (the younger the more desirable) compound an already complex situation that can only be addressed in the concrete encounter of living people.

African women also stake a claim for their own space within the discourse of women. In a fascinating work, Mercy Amba Oduyoye (1995) makes use of her Akan matrilineal heritage, Yoruba patriarchal culture (adopted through marriage) and Methodist Christian upbringing to offer an analysis of the lives of African women today. Her book is argued and illustrated with proverbs, sayings, myths and stories from Akan and other African traditional folklore and religion, in true African fashion. Mercy Oduyoye, a former Deputy General Secretary of the World Council of Churches, seeks 'to understand what the "daughters of Anowa" are experiencing today and where they are going.' She seeks 'the quality of life that frees African women to respond to the fullness for which God created them' (p.9). (Anowa is 'a mythical woman representing Africa': Armah 1973; Aidoo 1980.) She demonstrates how understandings of liberation for women imply the need for each group to speak for themselves and the pitfalls of any one group attempting to speak for all.

Black British women are also in the process of defining themselves as distinct from other women on the grounds of their own concrete social and historical experiences (see Jarrett-Macauley 1996). These experiences make them different from African American, African, Caribbean and Asian women. So that, while it is necessary to see commonalities between women's experience worldwide, any serious attention to the lived experience of any particular group will demonstrate differences that need airing and engaging with. Valentina Alexander puts it well:

In reality, the British Christian Black woman is extremely difficult to generalize about. Just when you feel that you have understood her most essential characteristics a new dimension emerges from the depth of her experiences, necessitating a fresh assessment. (Alexander 1996, p.85)

The importance of being wary of generalized statements about 'women,' 'men,' or even 'Black women' or 'Black men' for that matter, is clear. From the stance therefore of participating in and/or listening attentively to concrete experience of living people, we move, sometimes imperceptively, into joining persons themselves and other listeners in attempts at social analysis.

Social analysis

There is clearly a need for more social analysis in pastoral care and counseling. Social systems, although of importance to the pastoral theologian, have usually been of 'secondary importance in understanding individual behaviour, personal suffering and psychosocial development' (Chopp and Parker 1990, p.14). Pastoral carers need skills in scrutinizing the ways patriarchy, capitalism, militarism, sexism, racism, classism, religio-cultural ideologies and other 'structures' work in isolation or else in complex concert to initiate or aggravate the suffering of persons.

Liberation theologians understand human suffering to be directly linked with social systems that are oppressive to the human person. This systemic perspective leads liberation theologians to unearth and name the oppressive underlying social structures. The perceptiveness of liberation theologians could be greatly enhanced if, in addition to the socio-economic and political analysis in which they are versed, their ability to understand the depth of the psychological trauma which suffering people experience were increased. Why do different people experiencing a similar degree of social oppression react differently? What is it that enables different people to choose different strategies for dealing with oppressive family or social pressures? Why do some people feel so paralyzed by their social circumstances as to see no possible way out in spite of 'conscientization'? 'What happens when a mother comes to the liberation theologian crying because her husband has been violently killed in a protest march?' (Chopp and Parker 1990, p.17).

The devastating loss of self-esteem, the hopelessness and rage which fuels intrapersonal and interpersonal (e.g. 'Black-on-Black') violence, the despondency and despair in the suicidal person's eyes and the survival mentality involved in the prostitute's and drug pusher's trade – these require a psychosocial as well as a political and economic analysis. What is needed is not an 'either-or' but rather a 'both-and' in the analysis of suffering and oppression. Dialogue between pastoral carers and liberation theologians within an intercultural framework could result in deep psychosocial, sharp socio-economic and nuanced political analysis of the specific contexts out of which human suffering emerges.

Hermeneutical analysis

Pastoral caregivers like Stephen Pattison (1993) have commented on the 'strange silence of the Bible in pastoral care.' Questions have been raised and suggestions offered as to how the text may be appropriately offered in pastoral situations. With the shift in certain circles of Biblical hermeneutics away from the author's intention and the meanings inherent in the text, and more towards the reader's and their responses, with all the many dissenting voices, it would appear that some scope is appearing for a more 'pastoral' usage of the Bible (see Watson 1993). It is, of course, important to see these shifts in relative rather than absolute terms. A text is never seriously going to depend solely on the reader's response. A text will always maintain a degree of autonomy from its readers. It is this autonomy that necessitates interpretation in the first place.

However, there are significant ways in which the concerns of liberation theologians and pastoral carers can be served by a greater degree of attention to who the readers are, how they read the texts and what they do with them. Historical studies of what was done with the texts of the Bible in different societies, not least by missionaries in different cultures and by those who received missionary teaching, continue to be enlightening.[4]

As we have already indicated, Sri Lankan theologian R.S. Sugirtharajah, has done a great deal to enable the hermeneutical voices from the margins to be heard in the West (see Sugistharajah 1995). These are the voices of liberation theologians from across the Third World, and from marginalized groups in the United States, involved in hermeneutical engagement with the Bible and other sacred writings. Sugistharajah's *Voices from the Margin* is a veritable gold mine: from Zimbabwean theologian Canaan Banana's call for the revising and editing of the Bible, adding to it what is not there in order to liberate it and make it more relevant for today, through Trinidadian 'calypso exegesis' and Costa Rican women re-reading the Bible, one is struck by the serious and innovative engagement taking place between text and readers; Leslie Boseto of the Solomon Islands points out the relevance of the 'household economy' – where the household extends to members of the same language group (*won-tok*) – to the interpretation of scripture in the Pacific islands while Indian Muslim Asghar Ali Engineer, throws light on the developing liberation theology in Islam.

Also in *Voices from the Margin*, Kwok Pui-Lan of Hong Kong argues for 'dialogical imagination' as an alternative way of interpreting Biblical truth from an Asian women's perspective, which is different from the culturally imperialistic way of the missionary church. This is a critical and dialectical process through which 'Asian women discover from both bible stories and their people's stories the wisdom needed for their own survival and liberation' (Chung 1991, p.107). In dialogical imagination two trends are discernible. 'The first is the use of Asian myths, legends and stories in biblical reflection. The second is the use of the social biography of the people as a hermeneutical key to understand both our reality and the message of the Bible' (Kwok 1995, p.296).

Korean liberation theologian Chung Hyun Kyung proposes, innovatively and in my view very helpfully, that 'Asian women theologians should realize that *we are the text*, and the Bible and tradition of the Christian church are the context of our theology' (Chung 1991, p.111). She continues:

> Of course we Asian Christians must open ourselves to learn from the authentic collective memories of Jewish and Christian people in the West, but not to the degree that the latter become the totalitarian dictators in our world of spiritual meaning. The Bible becomes meaningful only when it touches our peoples' hearts, especially women's hearts that have been deeply wounded by the patriarchal teachings of the Bible. The Bible becomes a transforming power in our peoples' struggle for self-determination and wholeness only when biblical stories of liberation are re-enacted in our peoples' daily life. Then, and only then, the Bible becomes a living book for us.' (p.111)

This is the voice of a liberation theologian who wishes to bring a critical consciousness to the hermeneutical tasks, in line with the pastoral concerns of survival and healing for her specific people. Chung's point about people 'being the text' seems to me to be an important pastoral insight, arising out of a liberationist hermeneutic, not dissimilar to that argued by Charles Gerkin, in his pastoral classic *The Living Human Document* (1984), in which he follows and extends the pioneering work of Anton Boisen, founder of the Clinical Pastoral Education movement. In a collection of essays in honour of Gerkin's retirement from Emory University's Candler School of Theology, Pam Couture and Rodney Hunter (1995) write concerning this illustrious practitioner and teacher of pastoral care and counseling, that he 'developed...a sophisticated new understanding of pastoral counseling as a retelling of the human story in ways that expand social horizons and liberate persons from oppressive forms of consciousness and destructive patterns of interpersonal relationship' (p.9). Gerkin's later publication (1991) reflects his concern to critique society and 'change the common sense of the community.' The widening of the horizons of the theories and practices of pastoral care and counseling are moving in the direction of liberationist themes across the globe.

The pastoral praxis of liberation

How is liberation to be achieved? How is trauma to be relieved? Liberation theologians talk of radical social transformation brought about by drastic change within a situation of oppression. In Latin America, people have lost their lives in the struggle of those in poverty against those with money, power and influence. Practitioners of pastoral care, on the other hand, talk about painstakingly slow processes of excavation of thoughts, feelings and behavior that are self-defeating and interpersonally dysfunctional. Practitioners of pastoral care, in the main, would agree that individuals do change but they would argue that the process is often long drawn out and gradual. Radical transformation seldom happens.

Both views clearly have their limitations. What is called for in dialogue, therefore, is respectful listening with a willingness to explore one's own views of 'change' in the light of the other's. Frank Chikane wrote that

> The great achievement of EATWOT is that it has, during a dialogue which lasted a decade, exposed Third World theologians to realities of others which have had an impact on all, and it has made all of us more conscious

of forms of oppression in our areas which we had not taken seriously, and to which we were completely blind in the past. (Chikane 1990, p.166)

There are at least two levels on which the transforming dialogue implied in the process to which Chikane refers, may take place – the *pedagogical* and the *social-therapeutic*. Over the last 17 years I have been involved at both these levels. I shall end this chapter by suggesting two cyclical processes that have evolved over these years. The crucial thing in both is that they presuppose a multicultural group of people committed to intercultural encounter, learning and change.

Pedagogical cycle for liberative pastoral praxis[5]

There are five phases (see Figure 6.1) in the process I have adopted in facilitating learning within a group of people from different countries and cultures, of different ages, men and women, lay and ordained, of different Christian backgrounds as well as other traditions, with varying degrees of commitment to and challenge of their various heritages. Their only shared commitment is to learning for the purpose of being reflective practitioners of pastoral care in one form or another.

The process normally begins with *concrete experience*. Each participant begins the process in a practical placement situation that continues throughout the year-long period of study. This might be within a hospital, hostel for homeless people, hospice, community action project, health education program with 'working women' (in Britian, prostitutes are often referred to as such), prison, industry, counseling centre or other place where living persons wrestle with real-life issues. The main point is that it involves an encounter with people in the reality of life's experiences. The intention is to ground whatever theoretical discussion is engaged in, and there is a lot of that, in the lived experience of living people instead of the generalized and rarefied space of 'facts and figures.'

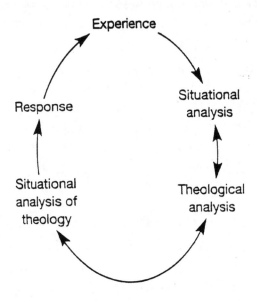

Figure 6.1 Learning cycle for liberative pastoral praxis

The second phase of the activity I have chosen to term *situational analysis*. This is an attempt to combine the social analytical mediation of Latin American liberation theology with the religio-cultural analysis of African and Asian liberation theology. Also involved here is the psychosocial exploration which pastoral carers and counselors tend to utilize. It may be described as social perspective taking. This form of analysis is multiperspectival rather than interdisciplinary. Instead of attempting the impossible task of bringing the full rigors of each possible discipline to bear on the situation in hand, various selected perspectives from different disciplines are employed in seeking a clearer understanding of the situation. The limitations of this process are acknowledged. It is suggested as an ongoing process that is introduced at this stage, to be continued in the life experience of participants.

To assist in this phase, experts from various disciplines are invited to comment on the situation. Historians, sociologists, economists, political scientists and psychologists could have contributions to make to the recognition of the complexity of the situation and the interconnectedness of different strands within it. It is recognized that each will, at best, be a limited view but that one of the best ways of gaining clearer sight is through 'collective seeing,' comparing visions and multiple perspectives.

The third stage is the point at which *faith perspectives* are allowed to question both concrete experience and situational analysis. Questions such as the following are raised at this point: 'What questions arise from my faith concerning what I have experienced and the analyses of it?' 'How has thought in my faith tradition approached the issues raised?' To be able to respond to these kinds of questions, reading and research is necessary. Participants look for standard as well as innovative responses to the issues from within specific faith traditions of their choice. They are also allowed to engage in their own personal exploration of the issues on the basis of their own faith understanding. They are required, though, to relate their own ideas to other recorded views on the subject. Participants are challenged to explore different ways in which an issue has been addressed in the tradition they choose as well as in others.' How has poverty, child sexual abuse or HIV/AIDS (or whatever the specific issue is) been written about and responded to in Methodism in different parts of the world?' 'How might it be handled differently on the basis of this tradition?' These and other such questions lead the way to focused theological study in response to specific lived experience.

In the fourth phase, it is my faith or tradition that is subjected to the *interrogation of the situation*. Here 'critical consciousness' is allowed to pose whatever questions appear necessary of the traditions of faith. 'How adequate is my tradition's formulation in responding to the concrete experience encountered?' I can vividly remember a session in which at this stage a participant enquired: 'How can a God who allows the abuse of his own innocent son inspire me to struggle against child abuse?'

In the fifth activity, the group explores the *response* options that are available to the participant in the light of all the stages that have gone before. Tentative decisions are made as to the preferred one. The participant will return and test this out in practice within the changed situation. Situations are never static. There is constant change in persons and circumstances. As such, one does not return to the same situation. Hopefully, one returns with new perspectives; one returns changed as one participates, with others, in transforming moments.

A cycle of social therapy

In Figure 6.2, I present a two-dimensional diagrammatic representation of a three-dimensional spiral process that seeks to bring together insights from pastoral care and counseling *and* liberation theology. It is a process that is informed at every point by the two disciplines, in an attempt to work for change within communities.

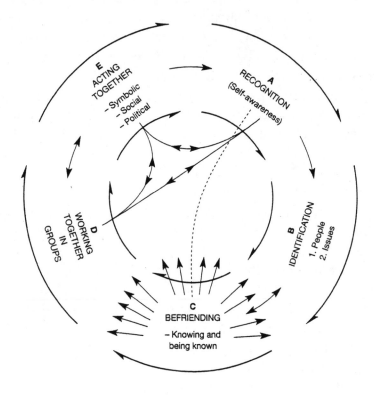

Figure 6.2 Social therapy cycle

One of the people who have been critical as well as involved in Christian social action is American practical theologian Dennis McCann, who has, quite correctly in my view, critically examined some of the dilemmas involved in Christian social activism arising from liberation theology (see McCann 1983; for a fuller discussion see McCann 1981).

McCann (1983) argues that there are 'two demons' that plague the efforts of Christian activists, namely, on the one hand, 'excessive spiritualization' and, on the other, 'politicization.' Each of these is an evasion of the demands of Christian social witness triggered by the 'ambiguous reality of social action.'

> 'Excessive spiritualization' does this by exchanging ambiguity for the certainties of a conventional *religious* righteousness – like the rich young man who went away empty when Jesus commanded him to sell all and give to the poor (Mark 10:17–31). 'Politicization,' evades the demands of the gospel by doing the same with an unconventional *political* righteousness – like the disciple who, when the woman anointed Jesus with oil of nard, protested that the perfume might have been sold and the money given to these same poor (Mark 14:3–9). (McCann 1983, p.109, italics added)

McCann shows how important it is for genuine dialogue, through the initiation and sustaining of structures of mutual accountability between the *communidades de base* (base communities) and the 'mainstream church,' to take place. The critique needs to be of both by each other. By reference to and in critique of the model of 'orthopraxis' proposed by Latin American liberation theologians, McCann suggests that 'orthopraxis' checks the tendency toward 'excessive spiritualization' only by promoting the 'politicization' of Christian faith. McCann prefers the older 'middle axiom' approach proposed by J.H. Oldham in 1937 and elaborated by J.C. Bennett, as more nuanced, reflective of the ambiguities of social action and more open to the realization that Christian social action may take a variety of forms both direct and indirect. McCann argues for the inclusion of Christian social ethics as an indispensable form of self-criticism in all Christian social action, recognizing that different kinds of critical reflection are required at different stages of social activity.

The model I am proposing attempts to avoid McCann's 'two demons' by including critical self- and communal analysis. What is envisaged is a model in which Christians as well as persons of other faiths may be not simply involved but rather *self-critically involved.*

I shall begin the discussion of this from the stage of *recognition.* A crucial starting point for any community involvement has to be a reflection and recognition of who it is that is becoming involved. I need a degree of critical self-awareness if I am to be involved with others. There are very many different exercises, approaches and disciplines for self-awareness which have been developed that can be gleaned within pastoral literature. From the various uses to which the Myers-Briggs Type Indicator has been put, through spiritual direction, introspective or directed retreats and prayer to therapies based on the work of different developmental psychologists. The point to be emphasized at this stage in this process is that it is necessary to have a sense of who the carer or liberationist, actually is as a living person. This process of self-awareness may be enhanced through work with another person such as a counselor, spiritual director, healer, therapist or *shaman*. The social 'actor' needs honestly to assess their strengths and weaknesses and to gain a sense of what particular abilities and characteristics they bring, together with a sense of what they are likely not to do very well in. They need to ask questions about what structures of personal and communal support they will have in initiating, sustaining and evaluating their activity. To become involved in communal action for change without this sense is to court disaster.

Having recognized, to an extent at least, who we are, the next step in the process is where an attempt is made to *identify*, first *people*, and next *issues*. The struggle for change is personal and political. Personal issues have political overtones. Political strategies affect persons. It is necessary, therefore, to find out as much as is possible about the people one is to be involved with in the community. Who are they? Where have they come from? How many are they? What demographic profile can be offered? This is a level of information about people that is best obtained by and from the people themselves. What are their concerns? What issues would they define as requiring attention? A question that is often raised in discussions of this phase is about the extent to which the pastoral worker can introduce ideas and identify issues *for* the people. Part of my response to that would be that if the worker becomes aware of any issues, it would be important that the issues be raised with members of the community to ascertain what it looks like to them. On no account should issues be foisted upon people. However, as a part of the next phase, within the context of discussion and issue-clarification, such matters may be fully aired and explored.

The third phase of the social therapy model spills over into the other earlier as well as later phases. It is not easy to define and restrict this phase to a particular moment in the cycle. The characteristic of the phase is *befriending*. Storytelling and story-listening are its constituent features. Caregivers and receivers, case workers and people are in a process of knowing and being known. Often, workers who do not wish to be known, who hide behind masks of professionalism, find that they are not let in to the complexities of social customs, norms, practices and problems that are present in all human communities. Those who are willing to become vulnerable, who risk being themselves with others, discover a depth of relationship and trust that others seldom even glimpse. There is an important interconnection therefore between the first stage of self-awareness and this all-pervasive phase of befriending. Befriending implies being prepared to risk one's very self to be in solidarity with others. From a Christian point of view, this is the heart of the gospel of the incarnate God who calls us to be 'imitators of him' (the phrase is Pauline, 1 Corinthians 11:1 reads 'Be imitators of me, as I am of Christ'). However, the dangers of befriending need not to be glossed over. These include the loss of a critical perspective and the diminution in the dialectic of distance-and-involvement discussed earlier in our considerations of empathy and interpathy.

Working together in groups on the identified issues and others that arise as the work continues, follows on in the cycle. At this stage, some skill and expertise in group work is helpful. There is a degree of task orientation that is needed. Groups direct their energy and attention by working on specific agreed tasks. The clarification of the tasks is a crucial aspect of the work of the groups. They must set themselves achievable goals and set in motion action plans that include means of evaluation and change of strategy. These groups may also provide the therapeutic support that individuals need for personal and social transformative action. Not all people within a community are equally able to engage in debate. The very nature of the groups to be formed, the manner of operation (language, procedure, etc.) of each group as well as the process of decision-making and dealing with the many voices present, needs to be dealt with in culturally sensitive and appropriate ways. In this cycle, every attempt is to be made not to silence any groups or individuals. When voting is resorted to, attention must be paid to those who are not the majority and as such do not 'win.' Ways must be found to ensure that minority voices are represented in the final outcome and decision.

The final phase of this model may also be closely linked with the previous one. There is a time when *symbolic collective action* is necessary and called for. Marches, protests and demonstrations are important ways of symbolically representing and calling attention to issues requiring attention. Political action, in different forms, may be the outcome of groups working together on issues of concern. This stage is linked with the previous one in another way. Symbolic social and political action requires support mechanisms. Groups in which people are known and cared about can be a valuable resource for support and therapy. Each person may find strength, encouragement and caution within the smaller group unit they belong to.

This then leads back to individual reflection and group evaluation. Symbolic action undertaken must be critically evaluated by both individuals and groups. There is, therefore, an inner dynamic and dialectical relationship between the first, the fourth and the fifth phases within this process. Individual self-awareness interacts with group work and with collective symbolic action in a constant, synergic and pastoral relationship that enables reflection, evaluation and support continually to refresh and refine the process.

I end this chapter with these open-ended cyclical models. They are by no means definitive finished products that conclude the search for methods by which pastoral care and social action may be brought closer together. Each model is intended to present one approach arising within the framework of interculturality, which provides some pointers as to how learning and action might draw on pastoral care and liberative praxis. In the next chapter, I shall be considering some of the crucial inter-relationships that exist between spirituality and pastoral care.

Notes

1. See Torres and Fabella (1978), a collection of papers from the Ecumenical Dialogue of Third World Theologians, Dar-es-Salaam, Tanzania, 5–12 August 1976; Fabella and Torres (1983), papers from EATWOT's first General Assembly, crucial for an understanding of developments in Third World theologies. Also very important is the tenth anniversary and Second General Assembly publication (Abraham 1990), which explores the common bonds as well as the distinctive elements within theologies arising from Africa, Asia and South America.

2. See Pattison (1993), Chapter 5 'Politics and Pastoral Care,' and a fuller development of this in Pattison (1994).

3. *Han* is a Korean word which has been explained to mean 'a sense of unresolved resentment against injustice suffered, a sense of helplessness because of the overwhelming odds against, a feeling of total abandonment ('Why has Thou forsaken Me'), a feeling of acute pain and sorrow in one's guts and bowels making the whole body writhe and wiggle, and an obstinate urge to take "revenge" and to right the wrong all these constitute' (by Hyun Young Hak, a Korean minjung theologian, quoted by Chung 1991).

4. For enlightening considerations of this, see Sugirtharajah (2001) and Dube (2000). See also, for example, from African Americans Felder (1991), Copher (1993) and Bailey and Grant (1995). A recent African exploration can be found in Bediako (1995).

5. For a summary of this process see Lartey (1996).

CHAPTER 7

Spirituality in Pastoral Care

Spirituality is an omnibus term. It means different things to different people and is notoriously difficult to encapsulate in a neat and comprehensive definition. Commenting on the meanings of the word in the west in the 1980s, William Stringfellow observes:

> 'Spirituality' may indicate stoic attitudes, occult phenomena, the practice of so-called mind control, yoga discipline, escapist fantasies, interior journeys, an appreciation of eastern religions, multifarious pious exercises, superstitious imaginations, intensive journals, dynamic muscle tension, assorted dietary regimens, meditation, jogging cults, monastic rigours, mortification of the flesh, wilderness sojourns, political resistance, contemplation, abstinence, hospitality, a vocation of poverty, non-violence, silence, the efforts of prayer, obedience, generosity, exhibiting stigmata, entering solitude, or, I suppose, among these and many other things, squatting on top of a pillar. (cited in Leech 1992, p.3)

The connotations of 'spirituality' are clearly many and varied, and they are not all equally attractive. However, the subject continues to generate tremendous interest among people in a vast array of disciplines and walks of life (witness the interest generated by Lyall 1995). How then are we to understand 'spirituality'? How is such a pluriform subject, which has been approached in so many ways, related to pastoral care and counseling?

On the basis of intercultural encounter and learning within the context of my own reflective practice of pastoral care and counseling, I shall indicate a structural framework of understanding for the term. I shall then, following an intercultural methodology, discuss the elements of the structure in detail with reference to voices from different cultures.

In the intercultural perspective I have been pursuing in this book, *spirituality* refers to the human capacity for relationship with self, others, world, God and that which transcends sensory experience, which is often expressed in the particularities of given historical, spatial and social contexts, and which often leads to specific forms of action in the world. In essence, our spirituality has to do with our characteristic style of relating and has at least five dimensions:

1. relationship with *transcendence*

2. intra-personal (relationship with *self*)

3. interpersonal (relationship with *another*)

4. corporate (relationships *among people*)

5. spatial (relationship with both *place and things*).

It is crucial to maintain that these dimensions should be understood as belonging together in an integrated whole. They are distinguished here for purposes of discussion, but in reality are inseparable. To escape some of the distortions that, I shall be arguing, are unhelpful, spirituality has to be understood as having to do with integration of the disparate aspects of being into a dynamic whole. In this respect, I find the statements of African-Canadian-American Peter Paris, professor of social ethics at Princeton Theological Seminary, most illuminating when he writes:

> The 'spirituality' of a people refers to the animating and integrative power that constitutes the principal frame of meaning for individual and collective experiences. Metaphorically, the spirituality of a people is synonymous with the soul of a people: the integrating center of their power and meaning. (Paris 1995, p.22)

I shall return to this synergic harmony between the 'individual' and the 'collective,' but what is of relevance here is the sense of spirituality as the 'integrating center' for an individual and a people. Nelson Thayer (1985) puts it this way: 'Spirituality is not merely inner feelings; it has to do with the integration and coherence of ourselves as experiencing and acting persons' (p.13).

It is important also to emphasize the relational nature of spirituality. John V. Taylor (1972) argued, in a seminal work on the Holy Spirit, that what is 'spiritual' about us is our capacity to relate. Joann Wolski Conn (1985), in a brief survey of some contemporary and classical sources, observes a common theme, with variations, thus: 'Relationship is the goal of spirituality and the pathways to it are means of developing and sustaining relationship' (p.41). Spirituality then has to be understood not in ultra individualistic and esoteric terms in which it has at times been characterized, but rather essentially as a relational term.

Spirituality as a vector quantity

In exploring spirituality, I have found a mathematical metaphor rather appealing. This is by no means to suggest that spirituality can be reduced to 'techniques' or to a form of functional instrumentality that confines it solely to practices with clear-cut results in view. In fact, in this understanding, spirituality is very much a matter of the warmth as well as of the foibles of human relationships. The mathematical metaphor I find helpful for spirituality is that of the *vector*. A vector, in mathematical physics, is a quantity that has both magnitude and direction. A scalar quantity, by contrast, only has magnitude. Thus a projectile (an object which is projected into space) has both speed and direction. It may be very fast, in which case its speed (magnitude) is great. But speed alone does not give a sense of direction of travel. Two projectiles traveling in opposite directions may have the same speed. It is the object's velocity (a vector) that tells us both its speed and direction.

Spirituality can be likened to a vector quantity precisely because it has both strength and direction. It is a dynamic concept that conveys the sense of travel, journey, search, quest, purpose or goal. At the same time, it manifests itself in terms of strength or weakness. On the one hand, we speak of its intensity or depth, implying by this that spirituality has variable magnitude. On the other hand, our spirituality can lead us in various directions. Vocation to serve God in a silent monastic order is a direction that may be very different from the call to take up arms and lay down one's life in defence of country or cause. This latter is also understood, as are other forms of martyrdom, as deeply spiritual.

'Spirit' and spirituality

To discuss spirituality it is necessary to go back to the root word 'spirit.' This word is etymologically related, in Hebrew (*ruach*) and Greek (*pneuma*), to the concept and picture of the stirring of air, breeze, breath and wind

(John Macquarrie (1992) points out that this is also the meaning in Latin, English, Sanskrit and many other languages). In Hebrew anthropology, *ruach* was the enlivening force of a person – the breath of God that turned the prepared clay into a living soul. In the second creation story in the book of Genesis, Yahweh breathes into the prepared earth, and the clay becomes a living *nephesh*. Thus the very being of the person is permeated by the *ruach* of God. This Hebraic concept of an animated body rather than a Hellenistic incarnate soul, which some have argued is the basic 'Biblical picture' (see Stacey 1956; Wolff 1974), has affinities with comparable concepts among many so-called primal peoples.

The situation in Greek thought leads more in the direction of a dichotomy between 'spirit' and 'body.' This split is most fully developed in the Gnostic developments of Platonism. Thus 'spirit' came to be identified with the realm of the eternal, the real, the ideal and 'body' with that which is corruptible and corrupting. What seems to be retained in Greek Neoplatonic mysticism, though, is the notion of a dimension of the human that is capable of participation in and union with the divine. Hegel, one of the greatest European philosophers of spirit, as Macquarrie argues, essentially agrees with the Hebraic picture refusing to 'isolate the spiritual from the physical and in seeing the former as the dynamic reality which expresses itself in the latter' (Macquarrie 1992, p.41).

Spirituality as relationship with transcendence

This aspect of spirituality is perhaps the most common and widely recognized. In the thinking of some people, it is the major, and in some the only, way in which spirituality is to be understood. In this sense, spirituality generally refers to the apparently universal human capacity to experience life in relation to a perceived dimension of power and meaning which is experienced as transcendent to our everyday lives, although such transcendence certainly may be, and often is, experienced 'in the midst' of our everyday lives.

The response and relationship with transcendence is most often mediated through particular cultural expressions within a given religious tradition's system of symbols. Such symbols include the language used to attempt to describe the nature of transcendence, the rites and rituals by which the relationship is initiated and maintained and the practices that are deemed appropriate for the strengthening of the bonds so established. Transcendence is spoken of as God, Allah, Mystery, the Ineffable, the Almighty, the Ultimate, the One, and in a host of other affirmations. In apophatic traditions, transcendence is approached more by a *via negativa*, in which it is not possible to affirm what it is. One can only recognize what transcendence is not.

The *nurturing* function of pastoral care is the one which is invoked by those who see pastoral care as being related to spirituality in this sense. Pastoral care exists to nurture spirituality. Thus practices such as worship; prayers for the lonely, the weak, the sick; preaching and visiting; are engaged in by the pastor in order to assist people in their spiritual journey. Indeed, the hope is that the journey would be enhanced and the relationship strengthened through these pastoral ministrations. There are very many manuals of pastoral care written to help train or form the pastor for such functions. The first part of Kenneth Leech's *Spirituality and Pastoral Care* (1986), especially the first two chapters, are written in this tone.[1] This is no doubt a necessary and proper understanding of spirituality. However, taken in isolation, and Ken Leech by no means suggests this, there is a danger of extreme functionalism and a focus on right technique which can be erosive of spirituality. There is also the problem of 'otherworldliness,' which may arise with this way of viewing spirituality. If what is ultimate, really significant and important lies 'beyond' this realm, then what we should be spending our energy and time on is not this world but what is transcendent. This way of thinking clearly leads to social and political apathy; although, as Ken Leech points out:

> otherworldliness in theology often manifests itself as extreme worldliness in practice, since it encourages a sharp division between the realms of spirit and matter, between religion and world affairs. Since the former cannot influence, question or shape the latter, they end up coexisting peacefully. (Leech 1992, p.15)

There is a traditional Ghanaian Adinkra symbol that has the Akan caption *Gye Nyame*.[2] Though extremely difficult to translate into the English language, it has been described as referring to the omnipotence and ultimacy of God. Mercy Oduyoye's (1986) statement captures the central significance of *Gye Nyame* thus: 'Without God nothing holds together; nothing has any meaning' (p.90). It is toward relationship with this ultimate 'ground of being' (Christian theologian Paul Tillich's oft quoted phrase) without whom nothing coheres, that African spiritualities would appear to point. This concept of transcendence seems to me to be one that may energize a holistic spirituality.

Spirituality as relationship with self

In psychological writings, it is perhaps in the work of Carl Gustav Jung that we find the earliest and clearest view of the importance of selfhood. Jung's therapy seeks to facilitate a process which, he would argue, could occur quite naturally. His therapeutic process, which he calls *individuation*, he translates as 'coming to selfhood' or 'self-realization' (Laszlo 1990). Jung chooses the term quite carefully because he is concerned to distinguish between 'individualism' (to which he objects) and 'individuality' (which he welcomes).

Individualism means deliberately stressing and giving prominence to some supposed peculiarity rather than to collective considerations and obligations. But individuation means precisely the better and more complete fulfilment of the collective qualities of the human being, since adequate consideration of the peculiarity of the individual is more conducive to a better social performance than when the peculiarity is neglected or suppressed (Laszlo 1990, p.148).

Kenneth Leech, in an award-winning book (Leech 1992), has shown how in contrast to the early 1960s when the word 'spiritual' was identified with escapist pietism and retreat from the needs and demands of the world, there is now a resurgence of interest in prayer, devotion, techniques of meditation and ascetic practices. Leech says that 'when Christians speak of spirituality, it is this inward quest to which they usually refer' (p.3). Leech is rightly alarmed at the confinement of spirituality to the realm of the private life of individuals. On such a view, instead of spirituality being seen as a way of living in every sphere, it becomes a sphere in its own right – 'the spiritual dimension' – and its contents and practices are exclusively a private choice which individuals make for themselves. Three aspects of this view give cause for concern – dualism, privacy and interiority.

Dualistic spirituality, as we have seen, asserts a sharp and qualitative divide between the highly valued 'spirit' and the less esteemed 'body.' Taken to an extreme, bizarre rites of bodily torture have been practiced to 'free' the spirit or to remove evil contaminations from it. Related to this is a separation of the 'sacred' from the 'secular.' This false separation fuels the kind of thinking, manifest among politicians when they are criticized by religious functionaries, that seeks to confine religious people to a sacred spiritual realm far removed from the real world of politics and economics.

When spirituality is a private matter it is entirely dependent on the individual. Leech argues that

> in traditional Christian understanding, there can be no 'private' spirituality. The word 'private', with its origins in *privatio*, robbery, is not a Christian word at all. Nor does individualism find any place within the spiritual climate of the Scriptures. (Leech 1992, p.5)

The Christian life involves being incorporated into a new community, a body, understood to be that of Christ.

The cultivation of the 'inner life,' Leech would argue, in the literature of the Catholic tradition since the sixteenth century, is seen as the main occupation of a spiritual elite called to advanced Christian living. Contemplative prayer, spiritual direction and meditation on the writings of the mystics are the hallmark of such cultivation. While Leech expresses a legitimate concern about the elitism and sociopolitical apathy inherent in an inner-life fixation, Nelson Thayer and Thomas Moore offer historical reasons for the 'loss of interiority' in the wake of the growth of scientific objectivism, Western consumerism and technological advancement and argue for the need in the West, for people to restore a proper relationship with the 'inner person.' Thayer (1985) argues that the recovery of interiority will include the capacity to pay attention to one's own experience in its particularity and richness. Moore (1992) offers a new way of thinking about the problems and creative opportunities of our everyday ordinary lives that draws on world religions, Jungian psychology, art and music. Moore's approach is a promising shift from an individualistic focus on self to an individuative embracing of soul.

The manner of the relationship we have with our selves is an important aspect of our spirituality. In traditional Christian teaching, much stress has been laid upon self-denial and abnegation. While self-denial is an important part of discipline, it has been pointed out that an insistence on it to the exclusion of all other Christian virtues has been damaging to members of oppressed groups, such as women already laboring under the burdens of low self-esteem. It is also true that such teaching was present with the slavers who forcibly insisted upon it in slaves while freely pursuing their greed for wealth and power in the name of Christian civilization. Healthy relationships with self require variable responses to particular characteristics of self. Those who are paralyzed by low self-esteem need to revalue themselves. They need a healthy dose of dignity, pride and a sense of worth. People whose self-esteem is so high as to border on inordinate pride need a realistic sense of humility and 'not to think of themselves more highly than they ought to.' Whereas the individual person is an indispensable unit, the person-turned-in-on-themselves can be self-destructive or destructive of others.

Another aspect of relationship with self has been described as self-transcendence. This happens, for example, where we are able to see ourselves and engage in self-criticism. In an illuminating piece, John Macquarrie writes of 'spirit' in the following terms:

> It is this openness, freedom, creativity, this capacity for going beyond any given state in which they [humans] find themselves, that makes possible self-consciousness and self-criticism, understanding, responsibility, the pursuit of knowledge, the sense of beauty, the quest of the good, the formation of community, the outreach of love and whatever else belongs to the amazing richness of what we call the 'life of the spirit'. And...though sin severely impairs this life, it never destroys it or humanity would cease to be. (Macquarrie 1992, p.44)

Human persons have the capacity to 'go beyond' themselves and their state. We can enter into critical conversation with ourselves. This is of the essence of our humanity. This openness may be and often is, directed toward another.

Spirituality as interpersonal relationship

The dyad is the starting point of the corporate. The ability to cultivate an *I-Thou* relationship with another person in which mutuality, respect, accountability and friendship are sustained, is indeed a spiritual task. Philosophers like Martin Buber made interpersonality the touchstone of their system of thought and living (see Buber 1970).

There is no I as such but only the I of the basic word I–You and the I of the basic word I–It. When a man says I, he means one or the other. The I he means is present when he says I. And when he says You or It, the I of one or the other basic word is also present. (Buber 1970, p.54)

For Buber, God is *das ewige Du* (the eternal Thou), the one who speaks to us. In this sense, there is an overlap between the spirituality of relationship with God and that which has to do with *another*. Much of the language of the mystics is the language of love, erotic in its longing for union with the Beloved.

The yearning for intimacy, closeness and indeed union with the 'other' that is the basis of sexual attraction, has furnished the vocabulary to articulate the mystics longing for union with God. In this language, 'spirit' and 'heart' – more prevalent in Eastern Orthodox Christianity – are very close. Thomas Merton speaks of the heart as the center of human personhood, 'the inner sanctuary where self-awareness goes beyond analytical reflections and opens out into metaphysical and theological confrontation with the Abyss of the unknown yet present one who is more intimate to us than we are to ourselves' (Merton 1971, p.33).

The devotion of the disciple to the guru, which we have seen is crucial in Eastern religious traditions, is an example of spirituality in its inter-personal aspect, even though the focus of the relationship is upon divine enlightenment and growth for the disciple. The union between woman and man in marriage, fraught, particularly in western Europe, Britain and the United States, with tremendous difficulty at the present time, is another example of this same form.

Spirituality as corporate

One can speak of the spirituality of a group of people. Obvious examples would be the various traditions we have within the different religions. We may speak of the spirituality of Franciscans, Carmelites, Dominicans, Augustinians; or of Methodist, Anglican, Jewish, Islamic or Hindu spirituality.[3] Within these would be discernible differences of emphasis and practice. These have to do with traditions into which persons are socialized and which have an influence on their patterns of prayer and relationships with others.

Similarly, one can speak of the spirituality of an institution such as a hospital, an agency or an organization. Here it may be the power of an ideology or 'mission statement' shaped by or shaping leading persons who then mobilize the 'workforce' in a particular direction. Gestalt psychologists take as their maxim the phrase 'the whole is more than the sum of its parts.' The power of corporate spirituality cannot be gauged merely on the basis of the individuals, even if they are leaders within the body. It would appear that the body acquires a life of its own, and its power for good or ill seems to have a force quite beyond that even of the founders.

African theologians have commented on the communal nature of African spirituality in ways that demonstrate the crux of the matter. Mbiti expresses this well:

> To be human is to belong to the whole community, and to do so involves participating in the beliefs, ceremonies, rituals and festivals of that community. A person cannot detach himself from the religion of his group, for to do so is to be severed from his roots, his foundation, his context of security, his kinships and the entire group of those who make him aware of his own existence. To be without one of these corporate elements of life is to be out of the whole picture. (Mbiti 1990, p.2)

Here the solidarity of belonging through participation is the mark of being. Religion is not a separate entity like the clothes we put on or take off at will. Rather, religion is like the skin we have – an integral part of our being – which cannot be removed if we are to remain human. In traditional African society, ritual commemoration is a binding force which expresses the communality of the spiritual bonds that tie people together. Spiritual movements are often sustained through the rituals in which members participate.

Spirituality as spatial

One of the most moving accounts of the spirituality of dislocated people was given by George Tinker, a Native American, at the Third General Assembly of EATWOT held in Nairobi in January 1992 (Tinker 1994). In his presentation, he refers to indigenous peoples like his own as the 'fourth world' discriminated against and exploited by first, second and third worlds. Tinker refers to Gutiérrez's introducing liberation theology as being a response not to the non-believer but to the *non-person*. He declares:

> Gutiérrez, like other Latin American theologians, explicitly identifies the preferential option for the poor with socialist and even Marxist solutions that analyze the poor in terms of social class structure and overlooks the crucial point that indigenous peoples experience their very personhood in terms of their *relationship to the land*. (Tinker 1994, p.121. italics added)

The crucial starting point of Native American peoples is their 'nationhood based on ancient title to their land.' Tinker's comments are to the point:

> From an American Indian perspective, the problem with modern liberation theology, as with Marxist political movements, is that class analysis gets in the way of recognizing cultural discreteness and even peopleness. Small but culturally integral communities stand to be swallowed up by the vision of a classless society, of an international workers' movement or of a burgeoning majority of Third World urban poor. That too is cultural genocide and signifies that we are yet non-persons, even in the light of the gospel of liberation. (p.122)

In Native American thinking, Tinker argues, all of existence is spiritual. Here the primary metaphor of existence is spatial not temporal. Spirituality is deeply rooted in the land, and that is why the dislocation of conquest and the forced allocation to reservations continues to be spiritually genocidal for Native Americans. This spatiality and land-rootedness manifests itself in ceremonies, symbols, architecture, world-view and views of personhood. Reflecting the revelation of *Wakonta* [Sacred Mystery, creator God] as *Wakonta Monshita* (above) and *Wakonta Udseta* (below) – Sky and Earth – the old villages were laid out in reciprocal halves. Moreover,

> each individual recognizes herself or himself as a combination of qualities that reflect both sky and earth, spirit and matter, peace and war, male and female, and we struggle individually and communally to hold these qualities in balance with each other. (p.125)

The fundamental symbol of Plains Indian existence is the *circle*, which signifies creation, tribe, clan and family. The circle is an egalitarian and non-hierarchical symbol.

Lakota peoples have a short prayer, *Mitakuye ouyasin*, 'for all my relatives.' Who are my relatives? – the two-leggeds, the four-leggeds, the wingeds, all living moving things, and also the trees, rocks, mountains, rivers, fish and snakes. The goal of Native American spirituality is the 'achievement of harmony and balance in all creation.'

The respect and reciprocity of relationship with the earth is a hallmark of Native American spirituality. The ecological movements often draw their inspiration from the beliefs, sayings and practices of these marginalized and multiply oppressed peoples. They constitute a very clear expression of spirituality as relationship with place, and with the things of the earth.

Pastoral care and spirituality

In the light of these considerations of spirituality, it would appear that pastoral carers, like others who care about people, will be involved in enabling themselves and others to be receptive and responsive to all the dimensions of life. Thayer's general statement on spirituality is helpful in drawing out the links with pastoral care:

> Spirituality has to do with how we experience ourselves in relation to what we designate as the source of ultimate power and meaning in life, and how we live out this relationship. (Thayer 1985, p.13)

Pastoral care then, may assist in our exploration of the dynamic journey that we are on in relation to ourselves, others, things around us, and transcendent reality. Such exploration may expose the demonic power (potential for destructiveness) of 'spirituality' when it is reduced and focused exclusively on one aspect alone. It may nurture an expansion of our awareness through engagement with unexplored areas of spirituality. Pastoral care may be of value in seeking an integration of our experiences and a centeredness that enables expansion.

Pastoral care, whether through worship, education, social action or counseling may facilitate an ongoing process of self-discovery, engagement with others and a deepening and broadening of one's discovery of relationship to, and participation in, the transcendent and the world community. No less than this is called for in an interculturally informed pastoral care.

In the following chapter, I present two case studies. The critical evaluation of the issues and challenges of response raised will demonstrate the outworkings in practice of an intercultural approach to pastoral care and counseling.

Notes

1. Leech begins thus: 'Christian spirituality is about a process of formation, a process in which we are formed by, and in, Christ: Christ who, sharing the form of God, assumed the form of a servant (Phil.2.6).'

2. Adinkra is one of the highly valued hand-printed and hand-embroidered cloths with origins in the Asante people of Ghana and the Gyaman people of la Côte d'Ivoire. Akan is the generic name for a number of ethnic groups (including the Asante, Gyaman and Fantse peoples) which share a common language, with different distinguishable dialects, and customs. The term Akan is used here to denote the common language.

3. As has been done in the 'World Spirituality' series under the General Editorship of Ewert Cousins. For example, Raitt (1989).

CHAPTER 8

Case Studies in Intercultural Pastoral Care

Pastoral care, as envisioned in this book, requires a broad and deep engagement with living persons in their universal, cultural and unique characteristics. It seeks to pay careful attention to the impact of each one of these three influences on every person. It calls for an approach that takes people seriously in their diversity, similarity and idiosyncrasy. Intercultural pastoral care has to be a corporate, cooperative activity in which the *many* work together for *each* and for *all*. Practitioners of pastoral care have to be aware of the symbols and signs present in different cultures and be willing to learn from each other about what caring for persons might mean in different contexts.

Two case studies are presented in this chapter, in which all names have been changed for the sake of confidentiality.

Case study 1

Okai was 42 years old. He had been married to Akosua for 13 years when, on the recommendation of a friend, he came to see me in my pastoral counseling office in an ecumenical church centre in Accra, Ghana. Okai and Akosua had a daughter, Ayele, who was 12 years old. They had tried in vain to have another child. Okai, a graduate in business administration of one of the universities in Ghana, was a manager in a large industrial concern in Accra, his hometown. Akosua was an Ashanti. Ashantis have a matrilineal system and trace their lineage through the mother, unlike the Gã (like Okai), who follow a patrilineal system. Akosua had spent much of her early years as a student in Britain, where she had first met Okai, who was in Britain on a short visit at the time.

Okai reported that his relationship with his wife had degenerated and was almost completely on the rocks. After a number of sessions of counseling, the origins and development of their relational problems began to emerge. Okai was not 'properly' married to Akosua, in traditional social and customary terms. His parents as well as crucial relatives in her family had not been in favor of the union. Together, Okai and Akosua had planned her pregnancy as a way to force the hands of Akosua's relatives. Akosua's maternal uncle, who should have been consulted, was left out and he died soon after the birth of their daughter. Since then, Okai and Akosua had fulfilled state requirements through a registry marriage in which legal papers had been signed and witnessed to.

In one of our sessions, Okai expressed the opinion that 'psychic' forces were at work trying to destroy the marriage. He had slowly come to this view as a result of recurring nightmares he had been having. In one of the dreams he had 'seen' his wife's maternal uncle standing angrily in a valley wringing his hands and looking rather menacing. When he had raised this with Akosua, she had wondered why a highly 'educated man' like her husband seemed to attach so much importance to dreams and African 'traditional superstitions.' 'Do you really believe that my dead uncle can do us any real harm?' she had asked. In the ensuing exchange of words, Okai had asked his wife why, if traditional beliefs meant nothing to her, she consulted 'herbalists and traditional healers' in addition to attending the hospital for medical attention, in the hope of having another child.

Okai offered the information that over the last couple of years he had been to see various religious leaders and groups, including a meditation group who chant and perform other Eastern religious rituals. One of the people he had consulted was a traditional healer who had reminded him that they had failed to attend the funeral of his late uncle-in-law. The traditionalist advised him to 'pour libation' and perform a rite of reconciliation at the tomb of his dead uncle-in-law. Okai had felt this was too 'pagan' and that such a deed would fly in the face of his Christian upbringing and faith.

Okai was clearly depressed, and had felt worried, tormented and harassed for quite a while. In our fourth counseling session, Okai declared,

'I did consider having an affair in the hope of having another child, however I dismissed the idea.'

'Why?'

'Well, I guess I was afraid.'

'Of what?'

'Well, I would feel really guilty, like I had betrayed Akos and everything.'

'Uh hmm?'

'Well... there is always the risk of infection – you can't be too careful these days – and, well, what if, you know I'm, erm..., or have become...you know, infertile?'

Akosua felt dejected and uncertain about what to do next. When I first met them together for a conjoint session, she expressed the view that Okai seemed to be losing control of himself. To which Okai responded by saying that he did also feel that Akosua had become distant and unresponsive to him.

Many of the criss-cross rhythms of present-day African life are discernible in this case. The interaction between traditionalist and modernist views of the world are apparent. The case illustrates the importance and relevance of an intercultural approach to pastoral care and counseling. In my interactions with Okai and Akosua, some crucial issues began to emerge and be addressed. I sought to relate with them as unique and precious persons who needed to be treated with utmost seriousness. We were confronted with African traditional views, especially concerning life, fecundity, death and the 'living dead.' Akosua's maternal uncle is a very significant figure in her matrilineal culture and family heritage. No counseling or pastoral care that does not enable them to explore these important cultural issues can hope to be effective.

What does it mean to remain childless after 12 years of marriage in a culture in which children are the 'sign and seal' of the marital bond? What are the implications of a belief, even a residual belief, in the 'ancestors as the custodians of social values'?[1] Is it possible that failures in interpersonal relationships can have consequences beyond the grave? Is it possible that the 'dead' can have psychic and personal effects on the social and psychological lives of living, to say nothing of their spiritual understandings and activities. These cultural questions become deeply personal in times of crisis such as they were experiencing. The question was: What do these things mean *for Okai and Akosua?* It is very easy and also most inappropriate to dismiss these perceptions as superstitious nonsense. An intercultural approach adopts the position that the perceptions and cultural concepts that influence people have to be taken seriously. These symbols and their perceived effects provide vital clues for the care and counseling needed. The impact of each strand of one's cultural heritage, while offering general lines of investigation, have to be teased out by and with each person. Okai and Akosua had to be assisted in working their own way through the different aspects of their cultural ancestry.

One central issue had to do with the nature of marriage in African society. Where should the emphasis be laid – upon the institutional or the relational dimensions of marriage? Okai and Akosua clearly cared for each other and had lived faithfully together, in spite of external pressure, for 13 years. However, they were not 'institutionally' married. They had not completed all the customary, ceremonial and legal requirements for a 'proper' marriage. Various expectations within the extended family networks remained unfulfilled. What is important is that, under the circumstances, the personal relationship was under much strain. Would these have been overlooked if they had continued to bear children? When is a marriage fully recognized as such? Questions were also raised about the nature of the marital arrangement. Is it best for marriages to be arranged, left entirely to the choice of the two individuals, or for some kind of consensus to be arrived at? In reality, in spite of a different emphasis in different cultures, there is usually some subtle or else overt form of interplay between arrangement, choice and consensus in most cultures. Okai raised and faced some hard questions about choices and commitments.

Akosua's allegiance to her matrilineage came under careful scrutiny. Within her Ashanti culture, she explained to me, 'marriage is friendship.' One continues to belong to one's mother's family. Married women, for example, do not take on their husband's name – that would amount to a loss of identity. She, under the influence of Western education and culture, had chosen on the one hand to reject this aspect of her heritage while on the other hand seeking to uphold traditional practices through consulting healers and herbalists. As such, she sought the benefits of both Western scientific medicine and traditional herbal treatment. In this way, she reflects both the conflict and the desire for harmony that lies buried within the psyches of people influenced deeply by different cultural systems. This conflict is played out daily in healthcare delivery systems in the 'Third World.' It is also evident in the growth of alternative medicine and therapies in the Western world.

Okai mirrors the guilt and paranoia often felt by those whose actions challenge customary cultural norms. Could his dreams reflect internalized symbols of his guilt, broken relationships, fear and anxiety over the consequences of failing to respect age-old customs? Could his attendance at a meditation group be an attempt to replace one set of fractured social relationships with other socio-religious practices? His apparent loss of control and fear of 'psychic' forces clearly point towards a rupture in the mechanisms of social and personal support by which he had been sustained over the years. This is most clearly seen in the breakdown in his relationship with Akosua, which had been a major source of support and stability in his challenge of the 'world.'

Gender dynamics are also at play here. The question of blame for the inability to have a second child weighs on Okai's mind. He worries whether it is himself or Akosua who is infertile. Apart from his apparent concern that guilt feelings might affect his relationship with his wife, should he have an affair, the paramount deterrent seemed to be the fear that it is he who cannot have a child. Okai shares the male ambivalence in traditional societies about culpability in such circumstances. This plays out in men displacing their anxiety onto their partners in terms of blame. Traditionalists advise men to leave their 'infertile' wives without seeking to discover whether the 'problem' lies with themselves. Okai could have had recourse to medical sciences for tests concerning his sperm count, as well as treatment if that should have proved to be the issue.

The conflict comes to a head when the traditional healer puts his finger on the heart of the cultural, marital problem and suggests a rite of reconciliation that aims at restoring psychic harmony between the players in this spiritual drama. Okai's objection surprised me, for it was couched in terms of a Christian faith in conflict with therapeutic rites he termed 'pagan.' Both Okai and Akosua saw little contradiction between their attendance at traditional or else Eastern religious ceremonies and their Christian faith, as long as such attendance did not directly challenge a loosely held Christian belief structure in terms of particular therapeutic practices. But there appeared to be a point beyond which they felt unable to go on grounds of faith. Among the many questions raised here were concerns about what practices, rituals and rites within a religiously plural environment were reconcilable with their Christian faith. How is Christian faith to be understood and interpreted within such a milieu?

In our work together, we came to a point where it was possible to explore some of the strands of this particular dilemma. We examined their understanding of Christian themes, such as eternal life and the afterlife; ancestors and exemplars of faith; meanings of health, healing, salvation and wholeness; the means of grace; marriage, family and community; guilt and forgiveness; and the cosmic significance of the work of Christ. The starting point was their own understandings and views. We then began working through the themes as they emerged. It was my task to offer some questions and insights from past and present Christian thinkers and writers from African and Western backgrounds. We examined the Western nature of the Christian belief structures they had been socialized into and attempted to raise African Christian alternatives that were equally compatible with the gospel.

As our work together progressed we found it possible to visit the graveside of the uncle. First Akosua and later Okai were able there to express their thoughts and feelings of hurt, sadness, sorrow and guilt. They were able to ventilate feelings of anger and frustration and to seek forgiveness and reconciliation. Together we ritualized their expressions in prayer and the casting of handfuls of soil on the grave. They found it possible to visualize Christ as the one who speaks from both sides of death. Christ enables forgiveness and reconciliation to be realized across boundaries of time and space. They found acceptance for themselves and for each other in the presence of God.

In one sense, the traditional healer's suggestions had been valuable for she had clearly articulated in culturally significant terms the crucial 'heart of the matter.' In another sense, it had been important for both Okai and Akosua to explore their own thoughts, feelings and behavior and to find themselves as individual persons within the complex web of relationships and cultural influences they were embedded in. The ritual brought together their Christian convictions with African traditional beliefs and practices in therapeutic and pastoral expression of forgiveness and reconciliation. Christ was both *person* and *symbol* of the harmony between the living and the dead, in the midst of the human community and with the 'powers' which they sought. The rituals at the graveside served as therapeutic agents that delivered spiritual and psychological relief in cultural terms.

Finally, we arranged a visit to Akosua's relatives in her hometown. In the event, the occasion was one of celebration and festivity, for it was perceived as a homecoming of a 'lost' daughter. Mother, aunts, uncles, cousins, brothers and sisters all became a part of a spontaneous outburst of joy and celebration. Some hard words were spoken. Tempers flared. There were times when I wondered whether anything would be achieved. One uncle was 'too busy in this harvesting season' to spend much time with the party. All told, a start had been made at the long and painful work of the healing of relationships.

Case study 2

Ayo, a 25-year-old woman, came to see me in Birmingham, England, because she felt the need 'to find clearer ways of expressing her feelings.' Her father is Nigerian and her mother is English. Her parents separated about five years ago. Ayo is in the process of leaving her mother, with whom she has lived since the family broke up, to live on her own. She has maintained contact with her father and visits him frequently.

Ayo's deepest sense of 'confusion' has to do with her cultural identity. The previous week she had been on a march in protest at the death of a young Black man in police custody. On her way to the procession, some white youths she passed called her a 'wog.'[2] As the march continued, a Black young man she was walking with turned to her and asked: 'Why are you out here in the cold, do you white folk really care about us?' Ayo confides that these incidents were not the first but rather an almost daily occurrence for her.

Although she has come to see me, she feels very hesitant about engaging in 'counseling.' On the one hand, she feels counseling is culturally unacceptable as a way of dealing with personal or family problems, since it entails, in her view, a betrayal of family bonds. She was brought up to be respectful of elders and authority figures, including parents. On the other hand, she feels the need to express her true feelings outside the complex network of family ties.

Working with Ayo was both painful and exhilarating. She was perceptive and had the capacity to explore issues, although at times progress was slow because she seemed unable or unwilling to be 'exposed.' Ayo knew what it means to be let down. She knew how to stand alone and to find inner resources to cope with appalling prejudice. In an early session, she confided that she had been smoking and drinking for the past four years but had felt it necessary to keep this away from both parents and close friends. She had began doing so on her 21st birthday.

We explored the themes of secrecy and exposure, guilt and shame from the perspectives of the cultures of both parents. It became apparent to her that she had internalized a value-system in which what was personal and related to family was to be kept hidden from any wider social or public view. This was the way in which her family (she had an older brother and a younger sister) had protected itself from the disapproving gaze of a prejudiced public. 'Personal' matters were best kept 'within the family.' There was now for Ayo a very solid dividing wall between what she would allow herself to discuss in public and what was private.

We explored the issues of self-expression. In Ayo's perception, her father had always expected his daughters to be self-effacing and 'in the background.' In spite of this, he had encouraged them to study hard and to become self-sufficient professionals. Education was the most important thing for them to have. At times, her mother felt Dad was 'too demanding.' Ayo felt the tensions of the conflicting expectations and survival mechanisms of her father. She had achieved a university education in languages and was fluent in French and Spanish. However, she felt unable to express her real feelings adequately. We explored her dress code and discovered a mixture of muted exhibitionism and a desire to blend in with others. Ayo felt, 'I cannot do what I want to do.'

'What do you want to do?'

'I don't really know.'

We discussed the close relationships she had formed and found that she had had fleeting relationships with a few men and now had a 'steady' who was also of 'mixed parentage.' She was, however, not very confident about how long this relationship would last.

To take Ayo seriously it would be important to allow her to discover herself as distinct from the significant people in her childhood and young adulthood. Her decision to move away from her mother's home was significant and encouraging in this regard. At the same time it was important for her to explore the influences within her that emanate from her father's Nigerian cultural context and her mother's English heritage. To do this she would need to be in touch with both parents and other relatives who might be helpful. Her moving was thus not to imply a severing of all ties with her past. Ayo had a thirst to understand her Nigerian roots. This is crucial for her health; for while she had had ample opportunity to explore her 'Britishness,' very little attention had been paid to her Nigerian heritage. In line with an intercultural approach, this desire was affirmed and encouraged.

Using the 'safe emergency' (to use an expression popularized by Gestalt psychtherapists) of the counseling setting, Ayo was offered the opportunity to try out various forms of expression of feeling in the imagined presence of 'father,' 'mother' and other significant persons. This was done using the technique widely utilized by Gestalt psychotherapists of imaginatively placing the persons on the 'hot seat' and speaking with them, and then assuming the hot seat and making responses to one's statements as one imagines they would. She explored what it felt like to be stubborn and disobedient to her parents. She expressed dissenting views freely and frankly. She 'replayed' situations in which she had been dissatisfied with her responses and tried out different ones. Ayo explored the boundaries of internalized 'culturally appropriate behaviors.' She gave expression to her feelings about the gender-role stereotypes with which she had been presented and the expectations which had been associated with them.

Finally, we examined questions about Ayo's identity. What does it mean to be a Black person who is perceived by some to be white? What does it feel like to be a white person who is seen as Black? Is one to be different in each social circumstance? To what extent is one to 'act the part' one is given? We recognized that these issues were the most crucial and painful of all she had been wrestling with. They fall squarely in the intersection of personal, sociocultural and universal human experience. Intercultural work seemed to enable Ayo to take significant steps in the direction of coming to grips with herself, in the midst of unresolved social and family conflict. Ayo reported that she had began to feel that she could be *any* or *none* of the persons she was called upon to be socially. She could be Ayo. She began the journey of self-discovery that is not about denying or excising parts of herself. For Ayo, her identity was to be found in exploring various streams and strands of heritage. These cultural influences were present within her. It was in exercising her ability to examine, identify, reject, embrace, accept and ignore these influences that she began to discover herself. Ayo reported a realization that her identity was multiple and that she was beginning to find that she could live with the complexity.

In the following chapter, which concludes the book, we will explore different approaches to pastoral care that are adopted in plural, global settings. The practice of an intercultural approach is further elaborated there.

Notes

1. For a very informed discussion of this, see Kirwen (1987), especially pp.26–54. See also Dickson (1984, pp.67–70).

2. A term of racial abuse in Britain.

CHAPTER 9

Approaches to Pastoral Care in Pluralistic Settings

Enhancement, not elimination of human diversity must be our goal. Diversity can be a source of harmony, rather than a source of conflict. Uniformity can destroy rather than advance civilization. A single world culture is not a desirable goal. (Augsburger 1992, pp.6–7)

In this chapter, we shall examine four approaches utilized by pastoral caregivers for working in multicultural communities.[1] Each approach reflects particular views of society and historical understandings of desirable sets of relations between people and amongst groups. Each enshrines and continues to reflect the chosen social vision and *modus operandi* of identifiable pastoral caregivers. Each is undergirded by theological and therapeutic assumptions that are more or less visible in the practice. Each seeks to offer effective pastoral care. Each has strengths and weaknesses that will be pointed out in the discussion.

Monoculturalist pastoral care

The monoculturalist basically claims to work in a 'colour-blind, culture-free' way. The basic anthropological and cultural assumptions can be subsumed in the maxim 'We are all really the same.' For such a caregiver, little or no attention is paid to differences that arise from cultural or social background. The overriding assumption is that all people in a given situation are basically the same. Cultural or social influence makes little or no difference to what we all are. Moreover, monoculturalist pastoral caregivers tend to assume that the therapeutic frame they choose to work with is suitable and applicable to all human persons.

Monoculturalist pastoral caregivers accept the presuppositions of the particular theoretical position that undergirds their approach to pastoral care and counseling. They proceed on the basis of these presuppositions, often with little cultural critique or social question. Seldom do they raise the question of cultural 'fit.' As such, they insist upon the core values and cultural norms of the particular class or social group for which the theory they espouse is most applicable. Most often, the theories they espouse have been developed out of research with members of that particular social class or group.

Monoculturalism as a social perspective, despite suggestions to the contrary, is not neutral. Three aspects of this non-neutrality are very clear, especially to those people who do not share the social and cultural assumptions of the practitioners.

First, the monoculturalist universalizes particular sets of norms, values, cultural beliefs and practices. Everyone, regardless of preference or background, is assumed or expected to function in accord with these universals. In this regard, the cultural norms of white Western patriarchal society and other similar cultures are regarded as the standards to which all must conform. In terms of pastoral counseling, for example, the tried and tested person-centered values of humanistic counseling, baptized with healthy doses of liberal Western theology, become the underlying premises upon which the practice of universal pastoral counseling is based. Similarly, in psychodynamic terms, object-relations theory, undergirded with self-psychology and reflected theologically upon through the lenses of Paul Tillich's theology, becomes universally applicable.

Second, monoculturalists at best deny and at worst suppress cultural expressions that do not appear to conform to this mould. This may be done through ridiculing or else rejecting the validity or theoretical rigor of approaches that differ from the preferred one. Any difference or divergence from the chosen approach is equated with deviance or ignorance and is denied, ridiculed, suppressed or forced into conformity. An example of this would be any form of counseling that would appear directive. This would be seen as inappropriate, oppressive or outdated. Practitioners of such abominable arts as 'advising' or 'informing' are shunned, roundly condemned or else offered courses in counseling skills.

Third, the cultural violence and coercion of monoculturalism is often not recognized by its practitioners. So firmly do they believe in the validity, superiority, strength and applicability of their theoretical frame that they are oblivious to the fact that others may actually quite seriously have genuine difficulties with it. There is an unwitting manipulation that accompanies monoculturalism.

Pastoral counseling in a monoculturalist framework has tended to take the form of an insistence upon privacy, intimacy, confidentiality and surrogacy. Such counseling usually takes place in one-to-one sessions held in the privacy of the 'pastor's office.' It is premised upon the ability of clients and counselors to self-disclose and to be articulate, autonomous, independent and self-directing – the predominant values of modernist, secular, Western society, based upon historic Western philosophy, psychology and theology. Much like the colonialists and imperialists in the age of European expansionism and the missionaries of a bygone age, monocultural pastoral caregivers pass on their therapies and value-laden activities as 'gospel.' These values are assumed to be normative in all 'civilised societies.' According to these therapeutic norms, any deviations from them are diagnosable pathological conditions.

Pastoral care under this regime places much value upon privacy and one-to-one counseling, and seeks to build up rugged individuals able to cope with the pressures of an alienated and alienating society. Through the use of personal counseling and small group interactions, professionally trained caregivers offer or else elicit coping skills from a clientele that is understood to develop through identifiable stages. Developmental theories are often the bedrock upon which therapeutic practices are based. As such, pastoral care is structured in terms of interventions or skills that are appropriate for persons at particular stages of development, these stages theorized by developmental psychologists and the clients having been diagnosed by therapeutically astute, trained professionals.

While the pastoral care and counseling described here is of great value for many in Western and westernized societies, it must not be assumed to be so for all in multicultural societies. This 'one size fits all' approach is quite clearly inappropriate in societies comprising diverse groups of people. There are those, even within Western societies, for whom this approach is wholly unsuitable. In terms of our earlier Trinitarian formulation (see Chapter 1), monoculturalists err through an exclusive emphasis on the 'universal' dimension (we are like all others). They fail to take seriously enough the cultural and individualist aspects of the threefold statement. The next approach to be described takes cultural difference more seriously.

Cross-culturalism for pastoral caregivers

Pluralism is the credo of the cross-culturalist. Cross-cultural work in counseling has been based on cross-cultural psychology. The latter sought, from its inception in the 1960s and early 1970s, to study and respond to cultural variations in behavior in a bid to validate or replicate generalizations about human behavior based on white European or American studies. Studies undertaken in Europe or America were suitably modified and then undertaken in other parts of the world in order to ascertain the extent to which these generalizations were valid.

Cross-culturalists recognize cultural difference. Such difference is located in social groups that are constituted on the bases of identifiable physical, geographical or cultural characteristics. There are three sets of ideas that seem to be uppermost in the thinking of those who take this approach to pastoral care and counseling. First, the very fact of *difference* – namely, the recognition that real difference exists between groups of people in a society; that we are not all the same. The most fundamental belief of the cross-culturalist is that they (those who differ culturally, racially or ethnically from us) are *totally* different from us. Second, cross-culturalists hold the view that the *boundaries* around groups are fixed, unalterable and, to a degree, impenetrable. Each social group is an entity within itself and needs to be understood and interacted with as such. Third, cross-culturalists assume that each group has an *identity* that is shared by all who belong to the group. Identity is viewed as a bond that associates all who share it. Group identity ties members together in the collective unity of homogeneity. Every member so identified is like everyone else within the social bond.

One of the pioneers of cross-cultural pastoral counseling is the American Mennonite David Augsburger. In a very useful book entitled *Pastoral Counseling Across Cultures* (1986) Augsburger argues for the need for 'culturally capable pastoral counselors' who have the 'ability to join another in his or her culture, while fully owning one's own' (p.19). Augsburger's aim is to assist in training culturally able counselors who are at home on the boundary. These culturally trained counselors are able to cross over effectively into another culture with deep 'interpathic' understanding and then return to their own. Howard Clinebell, in the foreword to the book, captures this vision clearly:

> Crossing over to another culture with openness and reverence and then coming back is the spiritual adventure of our time, according to David Augsburger. In his view, crossing over with this mind-set and heart-set enables one to return to one's own culture enriched, more aware, more humble, and more alive. In a real sense, the power of this book is that it can enable us as readers to cross over, experience a stunning array of diverse cultural realities, and then return home with the treasure and growth-in-personhood that comes from interpathic caring in different worlds. (Augsburger 1986, p.10)

Augsburger offers much that is of value and use in the encounter between cultures. However, there are fundamental problems that emerge when one adopts this mentality. First, is the difficulty that it encourages a 'them' and 'us' mentality that creates problems in any pluralistic society. It is *we* (invariably the dominant, white European/American) who cross over to *them* (the 'rest') and then return. *We* do things to them. *We* learn about them. *They* are different from us.

Second, is the unconscious assumption that the caregiver belongs to the dominant majority and the client/patient to the other. The problem is highlighted for me as a black African pastoral caregiver based in the West – am I part of the 'we' or the 'them' on such reckoning?

Moodley and Dhingra (1998) have recently commented usefully on the complexity of the relationship between counselor and client when the counselor is of ethnic minority extraction. Bearing in mind McLeod's (1993) reminder that counseling remains a predominantly white occupation with relatively few ethnic minority counselors, they explore the client's choice of counselor.

> For white clients the appearance of a black counsellor may unconsciously evoke certain prejudices and stereotypes which could lead to the rejection of the counsellor but be interpreted by the client as not having a right to choose. (Moodley and Dhingra 1998, p.296)

They examine white clients' strategies in accepting black counselors and black counselors' strategies in managing the relationship. By exploring the questions of 'race' in therapy and facing up creatively to issues of difference, perception and expectation, they argue that white client and black counselor 'can develop a rich environment for effective and creative therapeutic outcomes' (p.299).

A third very real danger in the cross-cultural approach is the encouragement of division through the *essentializing* of cultural difference. Essentializing occurs when we make particular characteristics the only true or real expressions of a people. The assumption is that there exists an authentic African, Asian, African-Caribbean or Black 'Other' who is totally different from the dominant one in every respect. The 'exotic' other only exists in the imagination and fantasy of the person within the dominant culture. This way of thinking leads to stereotyping and is related to an overemphasis of cultural difference. It fails to recognize the mutual influence of cultures within multicultural societies. Moreover, it does not realize that cultural similarity may exist across cultural divisions.

In terms of pastoral care, the identity and difference of the 'other' is recognized as sacred and advocated for by caregivers and counselors from the dominant culture. In British church circles, these brave souls become the 'experts' on 'the Asian community' or the 'Black community.' They then become spokespersons for these cultural groups and inform the rest of the dominant group, relieving them of any responsibility to get involved themselves in the difficult business of cross-cultural encounter. In one sense, these cultural informants vicariously bear the vulnerabilities of members of the dominant culture, who leave them to get on with it. Task groups or committees are often formed to deal with ethnic minority concerns. The members of these groups are then the only ones who really make attempts to come to grips with the beliefs and practices of the 'others.' From time to time, members of the subaltern groups who successfully manage to cross over in the other direction become incorporated as token representatives of their cultures and evidence of the liberalism, kindness and tolerance of the dominant group.

In the US, with its history of segregation, each racial group forms its own church and deals with issues on its own terms, respected (or despised) by the other group that moves away, hardly ever engaging in any real dialogue across racial lines. Pastoral care along such racial lines, has the potential to develop techniques and approaches that have the integrity of racial/cultural fit.

Cross-culturalism represents a serious and valuable critique of monoculturalism's presumption of universal values. However, it operates on the basis of an overemphasis on the identity, difference and homogeneity of cultural or ethnic groups. It must be pointed out, nonetheless, that in multicultural communities where subdominant racial groups have been forced to take up the logic of this position, they have managed to begin to develop more appropriate forms of pastoral care for their particular groups.[2] It would appear that in reaction to the violence of monoculturalism, cross-culturalist pastoral care enables the development of more authentic forms of pastoral care that respond to the needs and norms of culturally diverse groups.

While cross-culturalism overemphasizes difference, educational multiculturalism, which we will now discuss, oversimplifies cultural difference for the purposes of quick and easy encounter.

Multi-culturalism for pastoral caregivers

The fundamental premise upon with this approach is based is the need for accurate and detailed information to provide the basis for relevant policy and social action. If appropriate services are to be provided within a multicultural society, it would make sense for the nature and needs of the various cultural groups to be properly understood. Healthy 'race relations' within any community must be based on knowledge and information about the groups constituting the community. The approach to the multicultural society favored here is that of 'facts and figures' as providing the necessary tools for effective action. As such, an attempt is made to build profiles of the various ethnic communities in the society which seek to give information about, for example, social customs, religious rites, food habits, leisure activities, family patterns, gender roles, education and housing within each group. In Britain, in the 1990s, ethnic monitoring questionnaires represent, in a crude form, this approach to the multicultural society. This survey approach certainly goes a long way in providing information.

Problems begin to arise, though, when the information generated in such ways is understood in a reductionistic and individualized way. Then, such survey material becomes fuel for cultural, ethnic, religious or other forms of stereotyping. Stereotyping involves perceiving and treating any particular individual member of a racial or cultural group as bearing the presumed characteristics of that group. Stereotyping homogenizes groups, creating expectations of sameness among all who are classified as belonging to a group. Some attempts at multicultural education for counselors and pastoral caregivers, in an attempt at informing them about 'ethnic minority clients,' perpetuate stereotypical myths concerning, for example, the angry, underachieving Caribbean male; the Asian young woman's oppressive cultural role; the aggressive Muslim; or the problems of the Asian extended family system.

Along with categorizing often goes placing in hierarchical order. Cultural groups are tacitly, or at times explicitly, placed in order of preference or value on particular characteristics. In such rankings, the social or cultural group to which the one doing the classifying belongs usually comes out on top. Moreover, there is an accompanying presumption that particular cultures are fixed or in some way static. Canadian philosopher Charles Taylor, with reference to women, colonial subjects and black people, argues that the images produced by such listings of characteristics have the power to induce self-depreciation within the groups so described. Concerning black people, Taylor (1994) writes:

> ...white society has for generations projected a demeaning image of them, which some of them have been unable to resist adopting. Their own self-depreciation, in this view, becomes one of the most potent instruments of their own oppression. (p.75)

Multiculturalism adopts a commendable information-based, scientific data-oriented approach to the multicultural. However, like cross-culturalism, it fails to avoid stereotyping, reductionism, individualizing, placing groups in hierarchical order and perpetuating myths that, when imbibed, can induce self-hatred within the subdominant groups. Media, consumer, tourist, quick-fix or market considerations often lead multiculturalism. Busy pastoral caregivers wish to be able to obtain rapidly the information they need to enable them to visit or counsel their ethnic minority clients. So they turn to these manuals of information as they would to tourist guides. The problem is the gross oversimplification of the cultural, which can mislead and distort any real human relationships. Multiculturalism fails to appreciate the complexity of culture and, worse still, overlooks the reality of individual differences within cultural groups.

Such differences point to the uniqueness of persons within social and cultural groups. Overlooking this can be both oppressive and naive.

Pastoral caregivers who operate on such premises are often sensitive and caring persons who seek as much information as they can obtain in order not to offend or act inappropriately with the cultural other. However, what is lost in a dependence on this information is the spontaneity and sensitivity that is a *sine qua non* of genuine human interaction. 'For pastoral care to be real it has to arise in the midst of genuine human encounter where carer and cared for are both vulnerable and open' (Lartey 1998, p.49).

What is needed then is pastoral care that is informed by the material gained from surveys and statistical studies, but not determined by it. After the community survey has been done and the facts and figures ascertained, pastoral caregivers need to be clear that the work has only just began. They must understand that the study is not a substitute for genuine human encounter. They need still to approach any clients from the communities surveyed, with the respect, awe and wonder that all clients deserve. As all travelers to different countries know, the individuality and personhood of people and communities cannot be captured in surveys and tourist guides.

Intercultural pastoral care and counseling

We come now to the approach to pastoral care and counseling that lies at the heart of this book. As we have seen it is premised upon the maxim *'Every human person is in some respects (a) like all others (b) like some others (c) like no other.'*

In order to gain a fuller understanding of human persons within the global community, it is necessary to explore the ways in which culture, individual uniqueness and human characteristics work together to influence persons. The phrase quoted above (based on Kluckholn and Murray 1948) captures these three spheres of influence, which act simultaneously in the experience of every human person. By 'human characteristics' (we are *like all others*), I refer to that which all humans as humans share. This includes physiological, cognitive and psychological capabilities, with all the common human variations in them. The 'cultural' (we are *like some others*) refers to characteristic ways of knowing, interpreting and valuing the world which we receive through the socialization processes we go through in our social groupings. These include worldviews, values, preferences and interpretative frames, as well as language, customs and forms of social relationship. The 'individual' (*like no other*) or 'personal' indicates that there are characteristics – both physical (e.g. fingerprint and dental configuration) and psychosocial – which are unique to individuals.

These spheres of human experience interact constantly in living human persons who continually learn, grow and change. Intercultural pastoral caregivers seek to work with persons in the light of these presuppositions and realizations. Although the caregiving process is presented in three steps, these should not be seen as necessarily occurring in the order presented. Intercultural caregivers exercise flexibility and creativity in responding to need as well as promoting health. Pastoral care in this vein is not merely response to crisis. It includes creative health promotion through education, creative anticipation and community action. Let us now explore further the three kinds of issues attended to by the intercultural pastoral caregivers.

Like all others

As a therapeutic and communitarian necessity, there is an attempt to enquire what of the common experience we all share as human persons is to be found in the particular situation in question. The attempt here is in recognition and affirmation of the fact that all human beings are created in and reflect the image of God. The assumption, therefore, is that despite variations, ambiguities and differences, there will be evidence of humanity in all caregiving encounters. Intercultural experience helps us realize that no matter how different culturally or personally people are, there are features of their lives that resemble those of other persons.

Intercultural pastoral caregivers work to affirm the full humanity of all persons. People's experiences are held as human in all their complexity. In counseling as well as in community caregiving, intercultural pastoral caregivers work with people to assure them that they are human persons of worth, value and dignity, whatever their social, economic or personal circumstances may be. They work with people to establish those means by which their humanity will be enhanced and their flourishing promoted.

The pastoral caregiver who wishes to work in such an intercultural manner has to attend carefully to the common humanity shared by all people. He or she needs to face up to his or her own vulnerability in an open and honest way. There needs to be a leveling in which caregivers and receivers recognize each other as made in the image of God and reflecting that image in their humanity. Much in terms of recognition and respect of the other in their otherness needs to be acknowledged, especially on the part of caregivers who belong to or participate in dominant or historically oppressive groups. If there is to be any genuine human encounter, attempts need to be made to equalize the relationship through mutual awareness of power dynamics in such intercultural encounters.

Like some others

Intercultural pastoral caregivers attempt to figure out what in the experience being dealt with is the result of social and cultural forces. They pay close attention to specific sociocultural and socio-economic views and practices relevant to the social groups the care receiver recognizes as their own. What is encouraged is an affirmative as well as self-critical and open exploration of those cultural views and practices in an attempt to discover their influence upon the issue being examined. Within multicultural environments, the influence of other cultures than one's own will need to be investigated. No social group within a pluralistic society is unaffected by what happens to others. There is mutual influence between and within groups. Questions of power, domination, benefit and suffering are of particular poignancy here. Historical trajectories, as well as changes in power relations, gender dynamics and social class configurations, need to be attended to. As such, attention will need to be paid to differences and similarities that arise out of cultural factors. Here, knowledge and information about specific sociocultural, historical, economic and political matters of relevance to the cultures represented in the caring relationships may be valuable. But perhaps more germane to the process will be the exploration of the ways, as perceived especially by the clients, in which culture has in the past exerted and continues to exert an influence on the experience or issue in question.

Like no other

In intercultural pastoral care, attempts will be made to investigate what in the experience being faced could be said to be uniquely attributable to the personal characteristics of the care receiver. Questions will be faced as to what each person experiences uniquely. No matter how embedded one might be in one's social or cultural grouping, there will be characteristic ways in which one experiences or faces issues that will need addressing. It is important to explore issues of embeddedness, asking questions as to desirable degrees of freedom. Individuals are helped to exercise appropriate choices (i.e. choices they can live with) that are respectful of their cultural patterns of living whilst also giving them the desired freedom to be the persons they wish to be.

In an approach that comes close to what is proposed here, Lago and Thompson (1996) argue that multiculturally skilled counselors develop identifiable characteristics. Within a format reminiscent of Egan's three-phase model of helping processes and following the work of Sue and Sue (1990), they propose three stages in the practice of such counselors. These are, first, 'counselor awareness of own assumptions, values and biases'; second, 'understanding the world-view of the culturally different client'; and finally, 'developing appropriate intervention strategies and techniques' (Lago and Thompson 1996, p.136). The dimensions along which these develop are beliefs, attitudes, knowledge and skills. This helpfully provides us with a grid and a process to assist in the training of multiculturally skilled counselors, which, if used sensitively and not mechanically, can be of much use. In intercultural counseling, I have been struck often by the overwhelmingly positive response from clients who experience themselves as being taken seriously as individuals within their own cultural setting – respected as persons of dignity within their own cultural frame, with the integrity of choice to accept, modify or reject aspects of their heritage.

At various moments in any pastoral encounter one or other of these aspects of our humanity will be the focus of attention. Nevertheless, intercultural pastoral care will attempt always to have the other aspects in view and to hold all three in creative and dynamic tension. Here, a Christian Trinitarian and communitarian vision might prove useful. Making use of an analogy of faith, we can say that as with the distinct Persons of the Trinity, so with the features of our human experience. They can be and often need to be viewed and treated on their own in order to be taken seriously and more carefully attended to. Time and effort, for example, need to be spent discussing and exploring the nature of the Person of Christ. Nevertheless, the relational character of the three Persons must never be entirely lost sight of. In a similar way, the 'human,' the cultural and the personal in all human persons need to be attended to on their own while also being seen as in creative and dynamic interaction with each other.

Permit me to end by making four affirmations that I hope will shape and influence all pastoral care and counseling in the twenty-first century.

Pastoral care requires collective 'seeing, judging and acting

It was Belgian Catholic priest, Father Joseph Cardijn, a source of great inspiration to many Catholic workers and students between the two great wars, who originally offered Christians a way of more careful analysis of their circumstances by asking them to 'see, judge and act' upon their experiences (see Green 1990). This approach has influenced many in the Catholic justice and peace movement, liberation theologians in Latin America as well as Christian social analysts in the United States and in Europe.

The intercultural approach adopted in this book calls for emphasis on the collective nature of effective seeing, judging and acting. It is when many look at a thing through their own eyes and are allowed and prepared to share their visions that we may begin to see more clearly. We need the visions of many to critique each other mutually as well as to refine and supplement the monocular vision of one dominant person or group. Pastoral caregivers need the visions of many cultures on the issues they seek to respond to. The collective approach is required also in the art of 'judging.' It is where the many examine their evaluations that wisdom is to be found. To act reflectively together, socially and symbolically is to open the way for more transformative activity.

Pastoral care needs to undergo 'kenosis'

Pastoral care needs to go through a process of *kenosis*. By *kenosis* is meant an emptying of selfhood. In Christian understanding, Christ's 'emptying' of himself in the incarnation is the heart of the gospel (as celebrated in

Philippians 2: 5–9). *Kenosis,* in Christian understanding, is the character-istic of the life of the God who is constantly engaging in acts of self-giving. As we have seen, the term 'pastoral care' has its origins and selfhood in Christian thought and practice. We have observed that it by no means refers exclusively any longer to Christian activity. It is my view that the time has come for the essence of 'pastoral care' to be freed from the captivity of its 'selfhood' in terms of origins, in order that it can engage in real terms with the pluralism of the current world. Will it by so doing lose its essence and identity? I think not, for it is in such self-emptying that its true being-in-the-world may be realized. It is in giving away its very self that its truest goals will be achieved. Pastoral caregivers need the humility and trust in the divine presence that will enable us not to hold on tenaciously and obsessively to the symbols of office. Instead will flourish an 'other' directed practice that respects difference and seeks to give itself away in loving service. Such thinking is pivotal in inspiring the approach to pastoral care and counseling offered in this book.

Pastoral care is incarnational

Closely allied with 'kenotic' thinking, is incarnational theology. The presence and activity of God is to be found in the midst of the experiences of the world. This is not to deny the horrors of life in the world today that on face value might appear strongly to deny any such presence. Instead, it is to inspire the quest for redemptive involvement in the world. It is a call to all who care for persons and planet to become more deeply involved in the life of the world. It is a call to recognize God's presence in the various cultures and heritages of the world. It is to stand in awe of the mystery of 'otherness.' It is to engage together in a quest for clearer sight, for more incisive analysis and for creative, redemptive and transforming action for the integrity of each and all.

Pastoral care is contextual

Pastoral care arises out of and responds to the experiences of persons-in-context. The need for contextual analysis has been evident throughout this work. It is imperative that caregivers have an understanding of where people are really 'coming from.' Without this, the danger of retreat into the understandings of theories developed from outside their experience and into the worst forms of monoculturalism are very real. To take persons seriously means to make a genuine effort to tip-toe in their moccasins across the terrain they have traversed. The texture of the terrain is gauged in historical, social, cultural, gender, economic, spiritual and political terms. Pastoral analysis cannot be undertaken adequately in the absence of these features of the lives of ordinary, living persons. In point of fact, any true pastoral analysis of necessity includes all of these aspects. It is only when this holistic, contextual work is done that we begin to understand the stories people tell and to appreciate the reality they live. As such, pastoral care will look different in different contexts. The pluriformity of the creation demands this. God's creative genius challenges and calls us out of our lazy, monotonous repetitions of sameness into the rich color of the diversity that surrounds us.

Notes

1. This discussion draws on an earlier work in which I focused on pastoral counseling within multicultural societies. See Lartey (1999).

2. See for example Ed Wimberly's now classic text *Pastoral Care in the Black Church* (1979); also, Abraham Berinyuu's *Towards Theory and Practice of Pastoral Counseling in Africa (1989)*.

References

Abraham, K.C. (ed) (1990) *Third World Theologies: Commonalities and Divergencies.* Maryknoll, NY: Orbis.

Achebe, C. (1965) *Things Fall Apart.* London: Heinemann Educational Books.

Adams, J.E. (1970) *Competent to Counsel.* Grand Rapids, MN: Baker.

Aidoo, A.A. (1980) *Anowa.* London: Drumbeat.

Alexander, V. (1996) 'A mouse in a jungle: The Black Christian woman's experience in the church and society in Britain.' In D. Jarrett-Macauley (ed) *Reconstructing Womanhood, Reconstructing Feminism: Writings on Black Women.* London: Routledge.

Alves, R. (1969) *A Theology of Human Hope.* New York: Corpus Books.

Armah, A.K. (1973) *Two Thousand Seasons.* London: Macmillan.

Augsburger, D.W. (1986) *Pastoral Counseling Across Cultures.* Philadelphia: Westminster Press.

Augsburger, D.W. (1992) *Conflict Mediation across Cultures: Pathways and Patterns.* Louisville, KY: Westminster/John Knox.

Bailey, R.C. and Grant, J. (eds) (1995) *The Recovery of Black Presence: An Interdisciplinary Exploration.* Nashville, TN: Abingdon.

Ballard, P. (ed) (1986) *The Foundations of Pastoral Studies and Practical Theology.* Cardiff: Faculty of Theology, University College Cardiff.

Becher, W., Campbell, A.V. and Parker, G.K. (eds) (1993) *The Risks of Freedom: Pastoral Care and Counselling in Africa, Asia, Europe and North America.* Manila: Pastoral Care Foundation Inc.

Bediako, K. (1995) *Christianity in Africa: The Renewal of a Non-Western Religion.* Edinburgh/Maryknoll, NY: Edinburgh University Press and Orbis.

Berinyuu, A.A. (1989) *Towards Theory and Practice of Pastoral Counseling in Africa* Frankfurt am Main: Peter Lang.

Bhabha, H. (1994) *The Location of Culture.* London and New York: Routledge.

Billington, R., Strawbridge, S., Greenside, L. and Fitzsimons, A. (1991) *Culture and Society: A Sociology of Culture.* London: Macmillan.

Boesak, A. (1978) *Farewell to Innocence: A Social-Ethical Study of Black Theology and Black Power.* Maryknoll, NY: Orbis.

Boff, C. (1987) 'Hermeneutics: Constitution of theological pertinency.' *Voices from the Third World 10,* 2, 5–29.

Boff, L. and Boff, C. (1987) *Introducing Liberation Theology.* Tunbridge Wells: Burns & Oates.

Bohler, C. (1987) 'The use of storytelling in the practice of pastoral counseling.' *Journal of Pastoral Care 41,* 1, 63–71.

Bonhoeffer, D. (1954) *Life Together.* London: SCM.

Bridger, F. and Atkinson, D. (1994) *Counselling in Context: Developing a Theological Framework*. London: HarperCollins.

British Association for Counselling, (October 1991) 'Counselling: Definition of Terms in Use with Expansion and Rationale' (revised publication). London: BAC.

Buber, M. (1970) *I and Thou* (trans. W. Kaufmann). Edinburgh: T. & T. Clark.

Campbell, A.V. (ed) (1987) *A Dictionary of Pastoral Care*. London: SPCK.

Carter, R.T. (1995) *The Influence of Race and Racial Identity in Psychotherapy: Toward a Radically Inclusive Model*. New York: John Wiley.

Cassirer, E. (1995) *The Philosophy of Symbolic Forms* (Volume 1) (trans. R. Manheim). New Haven and London: Yale University Press.

Chikane, F. (1990) 'EATWOT and Third World theologies: An evaluation of the past and present.' In K.C. Abraham (ed) *Third World Theologies: Commonalities and Divergencies*. Maryknoll, NY: Orbis.

Chopp, R.S. and Parker, D.F. (1990) *Liberation Theology and Pastoral Theology* (Monograph No. 2). Decatur, GA: Journal of Pastoral Care Publications.

Christian, C. (ed) (1991) *In The Spirit of Truth: A Reader in the Work of Frank Lake*. London: Daron, Longman & Todd.

Chung, H.K. (1991) *Struggle to Be the Sun Again: Introducing Asian Women's Theology*. London: SCM.

Clebsch, W.A. and Jaekle, C.R. (1964, 1967) *Pastoral Care in Historical Perspective*. New York: Harper.

Clinebell, H. (1979) *Growth Counseling: Hope-Centered Methods of Actualizing Human Wholeness*. Nashville, TN: Abingdon.

Clinebell, H. (1981) *Contemporary Growth Therapies*. Nashville, TN: Abingdon.

Clinebell, H. (1984) *Basic Types of Pastoral Care and Counselling: Resources for Ministry of Healing and Growth*. London: SCM.

Collins, G.R. (1977) *The Rebuilding of Psychology: An Integration of Psychology and Christianity*. Wheaton, IL: Tyndale House.

Collins, G.R. (1990) *Christian Counselling: A Guide Book*. Milton Keynes: Word.

Cone, J.H. (1969) *Black Theology and Black Power*. New York: Seabury Press.

Conn, J.W. (1985) 'Spirituality and personal maturity.' In R.J. Wicks, R.D. Parsons and D.E. Capps (eds) *Clinical Handbook of Pastoral Counseling*. Mahwah, NJ: Paulist Press.

Copher, C.B. (1993) *Black Biblical Studies*. Chicago: Black Light Fellowship.

Couture, P.D. and Hunter, R.J. (eds) (1995) *Pastoral Care and Social Conflict*. Nashville, TN: Abingdon.

Crabb, L.J. (1976) *Basic Principles of Biblical Counseling*. Grand Rapids, MI: Zondervan.

Craig, G. and Mayo, M. (eds) (1995) *Community Empowerment: A Reader in Participation and Development*. London: Zed Books.

Culbertson, P.L. and Shippee, A.B. (eds) (1990) *The Pastor: Readings from the Patristic Period*. Minneapolis: Fortress Press.

Deeks, D. (1987) *Pastoral Theology: An Inquiry*. London: Epworth.

de Laszlo, V. (ed) (1990) *The Basic Writings of C.G. Jung* (trans. R.F.C. Hull). Princeton, N. J: Princeton University Press.

Derrida, J. (1976) *Of Grammatology* (trans. G.C. Spirak). Baltimore: Johns Hopkins University Press.

Dickson, K.A. (1984) *Theology in Africa.* London: Darton, Longman & Todd.

Draguns, J.G. (1989) 'Dilemmas and choices in cross-cultural counselling: The universal versus the culturally distinctive.' In P.B. Pedersen *et al.* (eds) *Counseling Across Cultures* (3rd edition). Honolulu: University of Hawaii Press.

Dryden, W. and Feltham, C. (eds) (1992) *Psychotherapy and Its Discontents.* Buckingham: Open University Press.

Dube, M.W. (2001) *Postcolonial Feminist Interpretation of the Bible.* St Louis, MO: Chalice Press.

Egan, G. (1986) *The Skilled Helper: A Systematic Approach to Effective Helping* (3rd edition). Pacific Grove, CA: Brooks/Cole.

Fabella, V. and Torres, S. (eds) (1983) *Irruption of the Third World: Challenge to Theology.* Maryknoll, NY: Orbis.

Felder, C.H. (1991) *Stony the Road We Trod: African American Biblical Interpretation.* Minneapolis: Fortress Press.

Foskett, J. (1984) 'Order and chaos: International Congress on Pastoral Care and Counselling, San Francisco, August, 1983.' *Contact: The Interdisciplinary Journal of Pastoral Studies 82,* 1, 21–25.

Foskett, J. (1988) 'Playing with one another: Some reflections on a visit down under.' *Contact: The Interdisciplinary Journal of Pastoral Studies 96,* 2, 9.

Foskett, J. and Jacobs, M. (1989) 'Pastoral counselling.' In W. Dryden *et al.* (eds) *Handbook of Counselling in Britain.* London: Tavistock/Routledge.

Foskett, J. and Lyall, D. (1988) *Helping the Helpers.* London: SPCK.

Freire, P. (1972a) *Cultural Action for Freedom.* Harmondsworth: Penguin.

Freire, P. (1972b) *Pedagogy of the Oppressed* (trans. M.B. Ramos). London: Sheed and Ward. (Originally published 1970 in Portuguese)

Fukuyama, M.A. (1990) 'Taking a universal approach to multicultural counselling.' *Counselor Education and Supervision 30,* 6–17.

Gerkin, C. (1984) *The Living Human Document.* Nashville, TN: Abingdon.

Gerkin, C. (1984) *The Living Human Document: Re-Visioning Pastoral Counseling in a Hermeneutical Mode.* Nashville, TN: Abingdon.

Gerkin, C. (1991) *Prophetic Pastoral Practice: A Christian Vision of Life Together.* Nashville, TN: Abingdon.

Gibran, K. (1980 [1926]) *The Prophet.* London: Heinemann.

Grant, J. (1989) *White Women's Christ and Black Women's Jesus: Feminist Christology and Womanist Response.* Atlanta, GA: Scholars Press.

Green, L. (1990) *Let's Do Theology: A Pastoral Cycle Resource Book.* London: Mowbray.

Gregory the Great, (1950) *Pastoral Care* (trans. H. Davis). Ancient Christian Writers no. 11; Westminster, MD/London: The Newman Press/Longmans, Green and Co.

Gutiérrez, G. (1974) *A Theology of Liberation: History, Politics and Salvation.* London: SCM Press.

Hall, S. (1981) 'Cultural studies: Two paradigms.' In T. Bennett *et al.* (eds) *Culture, Ideology and Social Process: A Reader.* London: B.T. Batsford and the Open University Press.

Hall, S. and Gieben, B. (eds) (1992) *Formations of Modernity.* Cambridge: Polity Press and The Open University.

Halmos, P. (1965) *Faith of the Counsellors.* London: Constable.

Harris, J.H. (1991) *Pastoral Theology: A Black-Church Perspective.* Minneapolis: Fortress Press.

Harvey, D. (1992) 'The condition of postmodernity.' In C. Jencks (ed) *The Post-Modern Reader.* London: Academy Editions.

hooks, b. (1981) *Ain't I a Woman? Black Women and Feminism.* London: Pluto Press.

Howe, D. (1993) *On Being a Client: Understanding the Process of Counseling and Psychotherapy.* London: Sage.

Howe, L.T. (1995) *The Image of God: A Theology for Pastoral Care and Counseling.* Nashville, TN: Abingdon.

Hughes, S. (1981) *A Friend in Need.* London: Kingsway.

Hunter, R.J. (Gen. ed) (1990) *Dictionary of Pastoral Care and Counseling.* Nashville, TN: Abingdon.

Hurding, R. (1985) *Roots and Shoots: A Guide to Counselling and Psychotherapy.* London: Hodder & Stoughton.

Hurding, R. (1992) *The Bible and Counselling.* London: Hodder & Stoughton.

ICPCC (International Council on Pastoral Care and Counselling) (1987) *Pastoral Ministry in a Fractured World.* Proceedings of the 3rd International Congress on Pastoral Care and Counselling, Melbourne, Australia, 19–26 August. Published by ICPCC.

Ito, T.D. (2001) 'The future landscape of pastoral care and counselling.' Keynote Address at the 7th Asia/Pacific Congress on Pastoral Care and Counselling. Perth, Australia.

Jackson, P. (trans) (1980) *Sharafuddin Maneri: The Hundred Letters.* London: SPCK.

Jackson, P. (1990) 'Spiritual guidance in Islam I: Sharafuddin Maneri.' In L. Byrne (ed) *Traditions of Spiritual Guidance.* London: Geoffrey Chapman.

Jacobs, M. (1982) *Still Small Voice: An Introduction to Pastoral Counselling.* London: SPCK.

Jacobs, M. (1985) *Swift to Hear: Facilitating Skills in Listening and Responding.* London: SPCK.

Jacobs, M. (ed) (1987) *Faith or Fear? A Reader in Pastoral Care and Counselling.* London: Darton, Longman & Todd.

Jacobs, M. (1988a) 'The use of story in pastoral care: 1.' *Contact: The Interdisiciplinary Journal of Pastoral Studies 95,* 14–21.

Jacobs, M. (1988b) 'The use of story in pastoral care: 2.' *Contact: The Interdisiciplinary Journal of Pastoral Studies 96,* 12–17.

Jacobs, M. (1992) *Psychodynamic Counselling in Action.* London: Sage.

Jarrett-Macauley, D. (ed) (1996) *Reconstructing Womanhood, Reconstructing Feminism: Writings on Black Women.* London: Routledge.

Jones, E. (1948) *Papers on Psycho-analysis.* London: Hogarth.

Jones, P. (1991) 'The promise of story for pastoral care.' Unpublished MA dissertation, Department of Theology, University of Birmingham.

Kareem, J. and Littlewood, R. (eds) (1992) *Intercultural Therapy: Themes, Interpretations and Practice.* Oxford: Blackwell Scientific Publications.

Kasonga wa Kasonga (1994) 'African Christian Palaver: A contemporary way of healing communal conflicts and crises.' In E.Y. Lartey *et al.* (eds) *The Church and Healing: Echoes from Africa.* Frankfurt am Main: Peter Lang.

Khatib, S. and Nobles, W. (1977) 'Historical foundations of African psychology and their philosophical consequences.' *Journal of Black Psychology 4,* 97–98.

Kirwen, M. (1987) *The Missionary and the Diviner.* Maryknoll, NY: Orbis.

Kluckholn, C. and Murray, H. (1948) *Personality in Nature, Society and Culture.* New York: Alfred Knoff.

Kwok, P-L. (1995) 'Discovering the Bible in the non-biblical world.' In R.S. Sugirtharajah (ed) *Voices from the Margin: Interpreting the Bible in the Third World* (2nd edition). London: SPCK; Maryknoll, NY: Orbis.

Lago, C. and Thompson, J. (1989) 'Counselling and race.' In W. Dryden *et al.* (eds) *Handbook of Counselling in Britain.* London: Tavistock/Routledge.

Lago, C. and Thompson, J. (1996) *Race, Culture and Counselling.* Buckingham: Open University Press.

Lake, F. (1966) *Clinical Theology: A Theological and Psychiatric Basis to Clinical Pastoral Care.* London: Darton, Longman & Todd.

Lambourne, R.A. (1995) 'Counselling for Narcissus or counselling for Christ?' In M. Wilson (ed) *Explorations in Health and Salvation: A Selection of Papers by Bob Lambourne.* Birmingham: Birmingham University Department of Theology. (Original work published 1969)

Lartey, E.Y. (1987) *Pastoral Counselling in Inter-cultural Perspective.* Frankfurt am Main: Peter Lang.

Lartey, E.Y. (1993) 'African perspectives on pastoral theology: A contribution to the quest for more encompassing models of pastoral care.' *Contact: The Interdisciplinary Journal of Pastoral Care 112,* 3–12.

Lartey, E.Y. (1996) 'Practical theology as a theological form.' *Contact: The Interdisciplinary Journal of Pastoral Care 119,* 21–25.

Lartey, E.Y. (1998) 'The Fernley Hartley Lecture. Pastoral care in multi-cultural Britain: White, black or beige?' *Epworth Review 25,* 3, 42–52.

Lartey E.Y. (1999) 'Pastoral counselling in multi-cultural contexts.' In G. Lynch (ed) *Clinical Counselling in Pastoral Settings.* London & New York: Routledge.

Lee, R.S. (1968) *Principles of Pastoral Counselling.* London: SPCK.

Leech, K. (1986) *Spirituality and Pastoral Care.* London: Sheldon Press.

Leech, K. (1992) *The Eye of the Storm: Spiritual Resources for the Pursuit of Justice.* London: Darton, Longman & Todd.

Lorde, A. (1984) *Sister Outsider: Essays and Speeches.* Freedom, CA: The Crossing Press.

Lyall, D. (1995) *Counselling in the Pastoral and Spiritual Context*. Buckingham: Open University Press.

Macquarrie, J. (1992) *Paths in Spirituality*. London: SCM.

Martyn, D. (1992) *The Man in the Yellow Hat: Theology and Psychoanalysis in Child Therapy*. Atlanta, GA: Scholars Press.

Masamba ma Mpolo, J. (1991) 'A brief review of psychiatric research in Africa: Some implications to pastoral counselling.' In J. Masamba ma Mpolo and D. Nwachuku (eds) *Pastoral Care and Counselling in Africa Today*. Frankfurt am Main: Peter Lang.

Masamba ma Mpolo, J. (1994) 'Spirituality and counselling for healing and liberation: The context and praxis of African pastoral activity and psychotherapy.' In E.Y. Lartey *et al.* (eds) *The Church and Healing: Echoes from Africa*. Frankfurt am Main: Peter Lang.

May, R. (ed) (1961) *Symbolism in Religion and Literature*. New York: George Braziller.

Mayer, J. (1989) 'Wholly responsible for a part, or partly responsible for a whole? An evaluation of the nursing concept of spiritual care.' Unpublished B.Litt dissertation, University of Birmingham.

Mbiti, J.S. (1990) *African Religions and Philosophy* (2nd edition). Oxford: Heinemann.

McCann, D.P. (1981) *Christian Realism and Liberation Theology*. Maryknoll, NY: Orbis.

McCann, D.P. (1983) 'Practical theology and social action: Or what can the 1980s learn from the 1960s?' In D. Browning (ed) *Practical Theology: The Emerging Field in Theology*. San Francisco: Harper & Row.

McLeod, J. (1993) *An Introduction to Counselling*. Buckingham: Open University Press.

McNeill, J.T. (1977) *A History of the Cure of Souls*. New York: Harper & Row.

Merton, T. (1971) *Contemplative Prayer*. New York: Doubleday.

Moodley, R. and Dhingra, S. (1998) 'Cross-cultural/racial matching in counselling and therapy: White clients and black counsellors.' *Counselling 9*, 4, 295–299.

Moore, B. (ed) (1973) *Black Theology: The South African Voice*. London: C. Hurst.

Moore, T. (1992) *Care of the Soul*. New York: HarperCollins.

Mosala, I.J. (1989) *Biblical Hermeneutics and Black Theology in South Africa*. Grand Rapids, MI: Eerdmans.

Myers, L. (1988) *Understanding an Afrocentric World View: Introduction to an Optimal Psychology*. Dubuque, IA: Kendall/Hunt.

Myers, L. (1992) 'Transpersonal psychology: The role of the Afrocentric paradigm.' In A.K.H. Burlew *et al.* (eds) *African American Psychology: Theory, Research and Practice*. Newbury Park, CA, and London: Sage.

Oden, T.C. (1984) *Care of Souls in the Classic Tradition*. Philadelphia: Fortress Press.

Oden, T.C. (1993) 'A response by Thomas C. Oden.' In W. Becher, A.V. Campbell and G.K. Parker (eds) *The Risks of Freedom*. Manila: Pastoral Care Foundation.

Oduyoye, M. (1986) *Hearing and Knowing: Theological Reflections on Christianity in Africa*. Maryknoll, NY: Orbis.

Oduyoye, M. (1995) *Daughters of Anowa: African Women and Patriarchy*. Maryknoll, NY: Orbis.

Paris, P.J. (1995) *The Spirituality of African Peoples*. Minneapolis: Fortress Press.

Pattison, S. (1986) 'The use of behavioural sciences in pastoral studies.' In P. Ballard (ed) *The Foundation of Pastoral Studies and Practical Theology.* Cardiff: Faculty of Theology, University College Cardiff.

Pattison, S. (1989) 'Some straw for the bricks: A basic introduction to theological reflection.' *Contact: The Interdisciplinary Journal of Pastoral Care 99,* 2–9.

Pattison, S. (1993) *A Critique of Pastoral Care* (2nd edition). London: SCM.

Pattison, S. (1994) *Pastoral Care and Liberation Theology.* Cambridge: Cambridge University Press.

Pedersen, P.B., Draguns, J.G., Lonner, W.J. and Trimble, J.E. (eds) (1989) *Counseling Across Cultures* (3rd edition). Honolulu: University of Hawaii Press.

Pilgrim, D. (1992) 'Psychotherapy and political evasions.' In W. Dryden and C. Feltham (eds) *Psychotherapy and Its Discontents.* Buckingham: Open University Press.

Poling, J.N. (1991) *The Abuse of Power: A Theological Problem.* Nashville, TN: Abingdon.

Pring, R. (1985) 'Personal Development.' In P. Lang and M. Marland (eds) *New Directions in Pastoral Care.* Oxford: Blackwell.

Raitt, J. (ed) [with B. McGinn and J. Meyendorff] (1989) *Christian Spirituality: High Middle Ages and Reformation.* London: SCM.

Archbishop of Canterbury's Commission on Urban Priority Areas (1985) *Faith in the City: A Call for Action by Church and Nation.* London: Church House.

Robbins, P. and Best, R. (1985) 'Pastoral care: Theory, practice and the growth of research.' In P. Lang and M. Marland (eds) *New Directions in Pastoral Care.* Oxford: Blackwell/National Association for Pastoral Care in Education.

Robinson, L. (1995) *Psychology for Social Workers: Black Perspectives.* London and New York: Routledge.

Rogers, C. (1975) 'Empathic: An unappreciated way of Being.' In C. Rogers *A Way of Being.* Boston: Houghton Mifflin Company.

Ross, A. (1994) *An Evaluation of Clinical Theology: 1958–1969.* Oxford: Clinical Theology Association.

Schlauch, C.R. (1985) 'Defining pastoral psychotherapy.' *Journal of Pastoral Care 39,* 3, 219–228.

Segundo, J.L. (1976) *The Liberation of Theology.* Maryknoll, NY: Orbis.

Small, S. (1994) *Racialised Barriers: The Black Experience in the United States and England in the 1980s.* London and New York: Routledge.

Stacey, W.D. (1956) *The Pauline View of Man.* London: Macmillan.

Steckel, C. (1985) 'Directions in pastoral counselling.' In R.J. Wicks, R.D. Parsons and D. Capps (eds) *Clinical Handbook of Pastoral Counseling.* New York: Paulist Press.

Sue, D.W., Bernier, J.E., Durran, A., Feinberg, L., Pedersen, P.B., Smith, E.J. and Vasquez-Nuttall, E. (1982) 'Position paper: Cross-cultural competencies.' *The Counseling Psychologist 10,* 1–8.

Sue, D.W. and Sue, D. (1990) *Counseling the Culturally Different: Theory and Practice* (2nd edition). New York: John Wiley.

Sugirtharajah, R.S. (1993) 'The Bible and its Asian readers.' *Biblical Interpretation 1,* 1, 54–66.

Sugirtharajah, R.S. (ed) (1995) *Voices from the Margin: Interpreting the Bible in the Third World* (2nd edition) London: SPCK; Maryknoll, NY: Orbis.

Sugirtharajah, R.S. (2001) *The Bible and the Third World: Precolonial, Colonial and Postcolonial Encounters.* Cambridge: Cambridge University Press.

Sugirtharajah, R.S. (2002) *Postcolonial Criticism and Biblical Interpretation.* Oxford: Oxford University Press.

Suzette, I., Speight, S.L., Myers, L.J., Cox, C.I. and Highlen, P.S. (1991) 'A redefinition of multicultural counseling.' *Journal of Counseling and Development 70,* 29–36.

Syed Hasan Askari (1980) Preface in P. Jackson (trans) *Sharafuddin Maneri: The Hundred Letters.* London: SPCK.

Symington, N. (1986) *The Analytic Experience: Lectures from the Tavistock.* London: Free Association Books.

Taylor, C. (1994) 'The politics of recognition.' In D.T. Goldberg (ed) *Multiculturalism: A Critical Reader.* Oxford: Blackwell.

Taylor, J.V. (1972) *The Go-Between God: The Holy Spirit and the Christian Mission.* London: SCM.

Thayer, N.S.T. (1985) *Spirituality and Pastoral Care.* Philadelphia: Fortress Press.

Thistlethwaite, S.B. (1990) *Sex, Race and God: Christian Feminism in Black and White.* London: Geoffrey Chapman.

Thorne, B. (1991) *Person-centred Counselling: Therapeutic and Spiritual Dimensions.* London: Sage.

Thornton, E.E. (1964) *Theology and Pastoral Counseling.* Philadelphia: Fortress Press.

Thornton, E.E. (1987) 'The absence of genuine community.' In M. Jacobs (ed) *Faith or Fear? A Reader in Pastoral Care and Counselling.* London: Darton, Longman & Todd.

Tinker, G.E. (1994) 'Spirituality and Native American personhood: Sovereignty and solidarity.' In K.C. Abraham and B. Mbuy-Beya (eds) *Spirituality of the Third World: A Cry for Life.* Maryknoll, NY: Orbis.

Torres, S. and Fabella, V. (eds) (1978) *The Emergent Gospel: Theology from the Underside of History.* Maryknoll, NY: Orbis. [128]

Trible, P. (1992) *Texts of Terror: Literary-Feminist Readings of Biblical Narratives.* London: SCM.

Tutu, D.M. (1984) *Hope and Suffering: Sermons and Speeches.* Grand Rapids, MN: Eerdmans.

Vankatwyk, P.L. (1988) 'The Helping Style Inventory: A tool in supervised pastoral education.' *Journal of Pastoral Care 42,* 4, 319–327.

Vankatwyk, P.L. (1995) 'The Helping Styles Inventory: An update.' *Journal of Pastoral Care 49,* 4, 375–381.

Vontress, C.E. (1985) 'Existentialism as a cross-cultural counseling modality.' In P.B. Pedersen (ed) *Handbook of Cross-cultural Counseling and Therapy.* Westport, CT: Greenwood. [23]

Walker, M. (1992) *Women in Therapy and Counselling.* Milton Keynes: Open University Press.

Watson, F. (ed) (1993) *The Open Text: New Directions for Biblical Studies?* London: SCM.

West, C. (1981) 'North American Blacks.' In S. Torres and J. Eagleson (eds) *The Challenge of Basic Christian Communities*. Maryknoll, NY: Orbis.

Williams, R. (2002) *Writing in the Dust: After September 11th*. Grand Rapids, MI and Cambridge, UK: Eerdmans.

Wilson, M.J. (1988) *A Coat of Many Colours: Pastoral Studies of the Christian Way of Life*. London: Epworth Press.

Wimberly, E.P. (1979) *Pastoral Care in the Black Church*. Nashville, TN: Abingdon.

Wimberly, E.P. (1991) *African American Pastoral Care*. Nashville, TN: Abingdon.

Wimberly, E.P. and Wimberly, A.S. (1986) *Liberation and Human Wholeness*. Nashville, TN: Abingdon.

Wolff, H.W. (1974) *Anthropology of the Old Testament*. London: SCM.

Woods, T. (1999) *Beginning Postmodernism*. Manchester and New York: Manchester University Press.

Wright, F. (1980) *The Pastoral Nature of Ministry*. London: SCM.

Subject Index

Author index

Abraham, K. C. 138n
Abu Tawwama 48
Achebe, C. 40
Adams, J. E. 105
Adler, A. 83
Aidoo, A. A. 126
Alexander, V. 126–7
Alves, R. 113
Ambrose, St 46
Arles, N. 53
Armah, A. K. 126
Assagioli, R. 87
Augsburger, D. W. 34, 35–6, 41n, 65–6,
    93–4, 99, 163, 164, 166–7
Augustine, St 46

Bailey, R. C. and Grant, J. 139n
Banana, C. 128–9
Barnett-Cowan, A. 52–3
Baxter, R. 46
Becher, W., Campbell, A. V. and Parker, G. K.
    50
Beck, A. 84
Bediako, K. 139n
Bennett, J. C. 135
Berinyuu, A. A. 24, 25, 72, 177n
Berne, E. 85
Bhabha, H. 40
Billington, R., Strawbridge, S., Greenside, L.
    and Fitzsimons, A. 31
Boesak, A. 116
Boff, C. 121
Boff, L. and Boff, C. 57–8, 114, 115, 118,
    119, 122
Bohler, C. 72, 73
Boisen, A. 130
Bonaventura, St 46
Bonhoeffer, D. 89–90
Bonsi, E. 53–4
Boseto, L. 129
Bridger, F. and Atkinson, D. 106
British Association for Counselling (BAC) 82,
    83
Brito, J. C. 52
Bu Calendar of Pinniped 48
Buber, M. 147–8

Campbell, A. V. 23, 50
Cardijn, Father Joseph 175

Carkhuff 111n
Carter, R. T. 96
Cassian, J. 47
Cassirer, E. 76
Chanona, C. 51
Chenchiah, P. 121
Chikane, F. 119, 130–1
Chopp, R. S. and Parker, D. F. 127
Christian, C. 111n
Chrysostom, St John 46
Chung, A. L. C. 121
Chung, H. K. 124, 125, 129–30, 139n
Cicero 43
Clebsch, W. A. and Jaekle, C. R. 21, 44, 62,
    81
Clinebell, H. 22–3, 62, 66, 87, 103, 167
Collins, G. R. 105–6
Cone, J. H. 113
Conn, J. W. 141–2
Constantine, Emperor 44
Copher, C. B. 139n
Couture, P. D. and Hunter, R. J. 130
Crabb, L. J. 106
Craig, G. and Mayo, M. 68
Crantor 43
Culbertson, P. L. and Shippee, A. B. 45
Cyprian, St 46

Davis, H. 46
Deeks, D. 61, 72
Derrida, J. 39
Dickson, K. A. 162n
Draguns, J. G. 35
Dryden, W. and Feltham, C. 108–9
Dube, M. W. 139n
Dudden, F. H. 46

Egan, G. 92, 100, 101–2, 111n
Ellis, A. 84
Engineer, A. A. 129

Fabella, V. and Torres, C. 138n
Felder, C. H. 139n
Foskett, J. 51
Foskett, J. and Jacobs, M. 104
Foskett, J. and Lyall, D. 72–3
Foucault, M. 39
Frank, J. D. 25
Frankl, V. 87
Freire, P. 58
Freud, S. 75, 83, 97
Friedman, E. 52
Fukuyama, M. A. 35